A Book of Trees
by

Stephen   Hanson

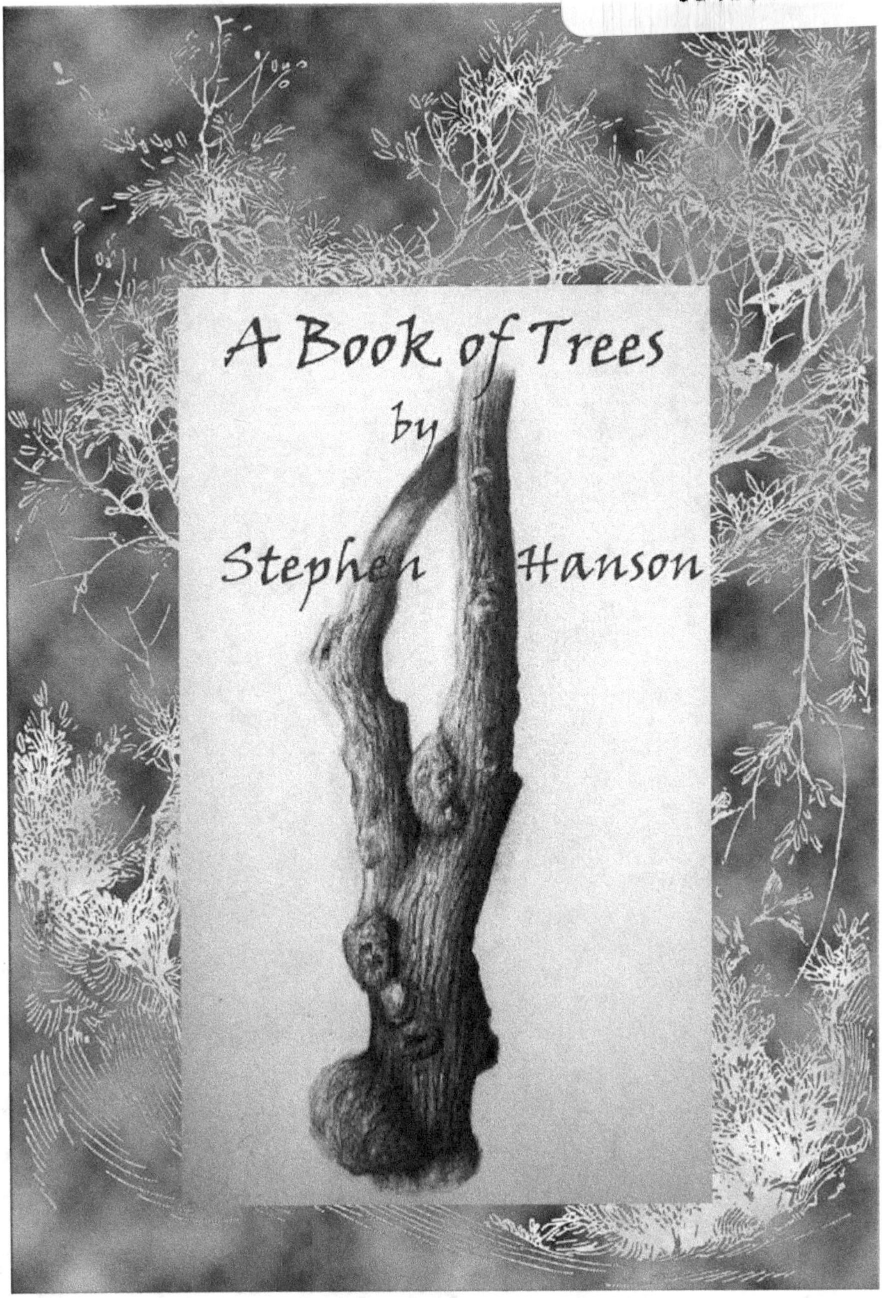

ISBN: 1984201476

ISBN-13: 9781984201478

DEDICATION

This book is dedicated to all who love and can appreciate the beauty of a tree and see its significance in a world filled full of hate and violence.

INTRODUCTION

1/17/18

I've always been attracted to the beauty and character of a tree. There is such a wide variety of different types of trees all around us that a person could spend a life time documenting the different types and species of them.

Over the last several years I would always be drawing something that attracted my attention and usually it would be a tree of some sort. Typically the ones that had twisting branches and other striking features would fill me with the most interest.

In the past I used some of these drawings to adorn the pages of previous volumes I had written, but now I decided that perhaps I should also do a book about the very thing that I often have drawn. There are other books that have been published that show beautiful photographs about various types of trees, and there are also how-to books that have been written for those who want to know how to draw a tree. But I would venture to say that this type of book is something of a rarity.

Each tree seems to symbolize a thing of great character and endurance to me. As it spreads forth its limbs and branches I see it as it reaches to the sun for its growth and strength. There seems to be as many varieties of trees as there are people, and each one is individual in its own right. This book is divided up into several sections of types of drawings of trees that have been of interest to me over the last several years. During the day I have often chosen to draw something and more often than not, it was a tree of some sort.

While most of these drawings are realistic in appearance, my inspiration has also spread to creating designs from limbs and trunks and adding other elements along with what was originally just a simple sketch of a tree.

It has been said by others that drawing is the foundation of the visual arts and I believe this to be true. For when one excels at drawing then this skill can be applied to painting, sculpture, and any of the other arts. Perhaps a drawing may not seem to be held in such high regard as a painting, but I believe that the qualities found in it can be considered as a finished piece of art as well.

I continue to paint landscapes and other subject matter, but drawing will always be a continued pursuit of mine and something that I will always enjoy doing.

This will probably be a life long journey of mine, because in my walks and observations, I will keep seeing new and unusual trees around me. My hope is that this little book will give you some small pleasure and that you will join in with me as we see the beauty of nature around us in the form of trees.

Stephen Hanson

CONTENTS

A BOOK OF TREES

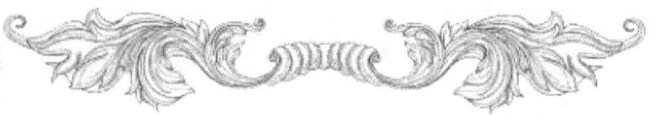

SEASONS

Several years ago I decided to do a few drawings of the various seasons of a tree. I thought that this type of thing would be a good thing to show how the character and the image of a tree would go through the changes that are so evident during the four cycles of the year.

I never get tired of seeing the differences that are displayed in these seasons because each one is unique. Certain seasons don't always have a clear beginning and an end point, but as one is patient in their observations, they will see clear demarcations in how foliage and blooms arrive and how their coloring changes and eventually decays and falls to the ground.

One can perhaps more easily depict a change in the seasons in a painting because of the choice of different colors and hues. Hopefully I have shown these changes through the use of the renderings that I have done in pencil.

I believe that these four seasons also have merit for us as people, as we also go through seasons in our own lives. Each season has a distinct look that is seen as the buds begin to be seen on the branches, as leaves begin to form and grow, as they turn colors and finally fall to the ground, and eventually become barren.

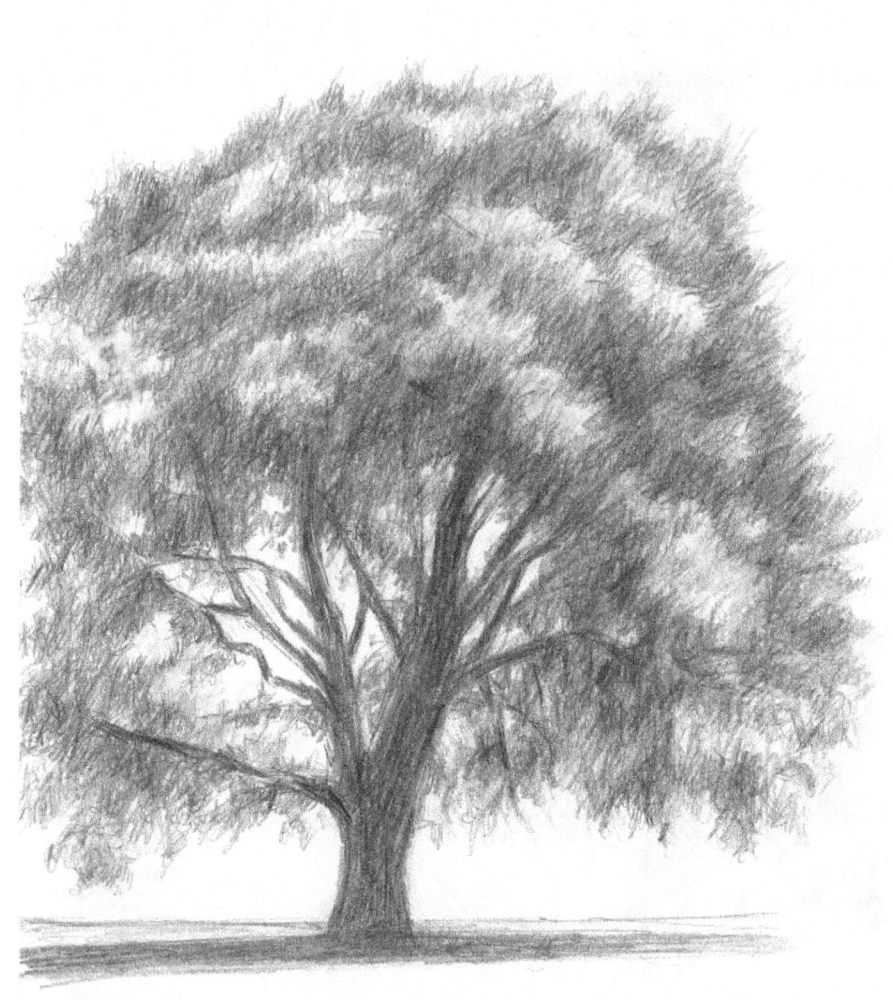

There are of course different seasons that one would see a tree in. There is a winter, a spring, a summer and a fall, where one would see the very same tree, but its very character would take on different colors and in this process, would lose and begin the process of forming new life once again. The drawing above is a tree I saw near me during the summer months. Although one cannot see the various colors, its leaves are full reaching upwards to the sun's light.

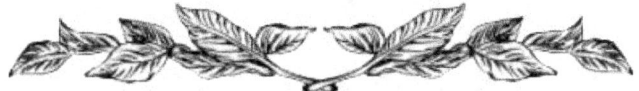

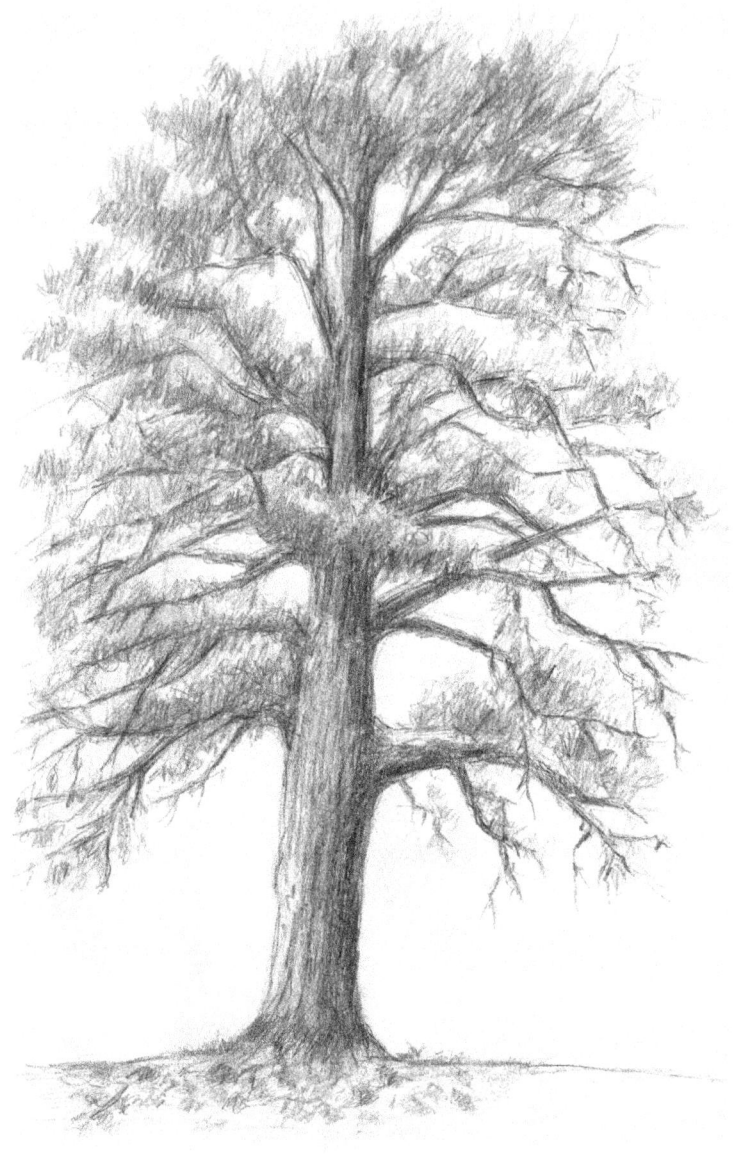

The tree as shown on the previous page is during the autumn months. While this one is of a Ponderosa Pine, one can see the fallen leaves and twigs below on the ground. The autumn months are filled with other hues and colors. There are browns and golds and muted crimson colors all adorning the leaves of many different types of trees. It is a time of reflection and looking back at the previous seasons of the year.

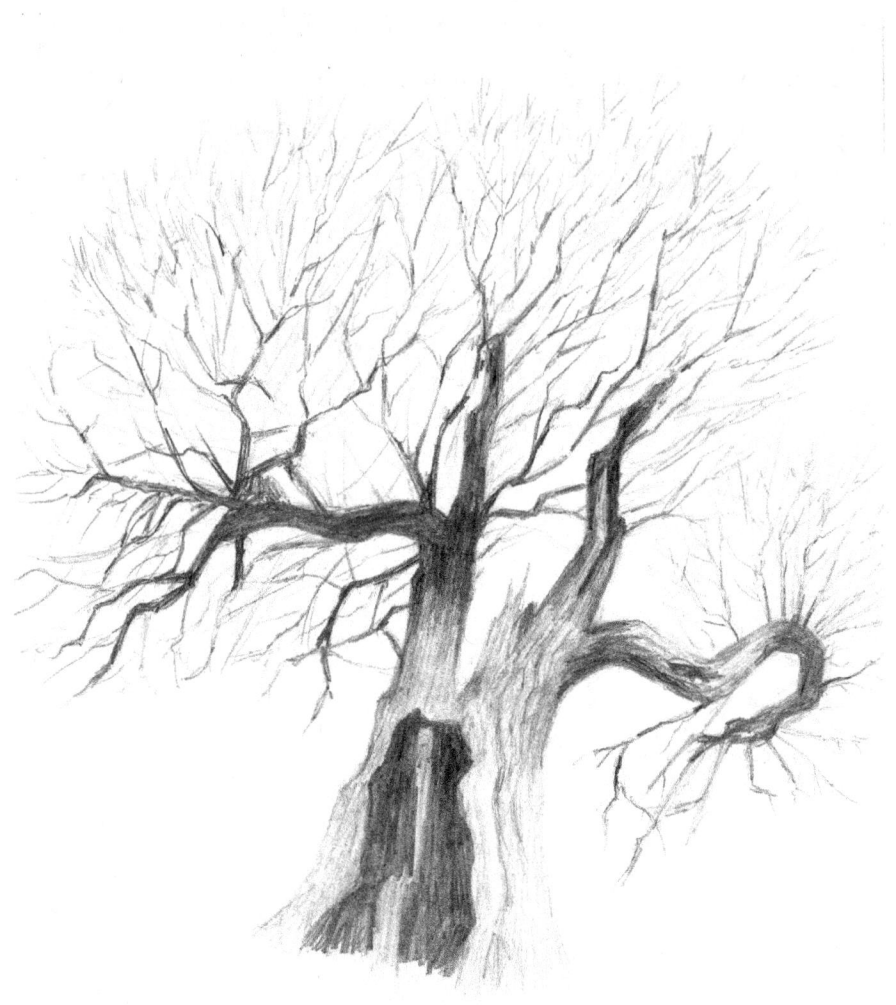

During the winter months the trees become barren and are seemingly devoid of life. But deep down inside as they weather the cold temperatures and winds, they are strengthening their roots and drawing nurture from the deep. This old tree may look very weathered and torn, but it has stood the test of time and can still stand when the cold, winter winds come against it.

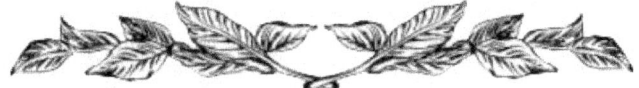

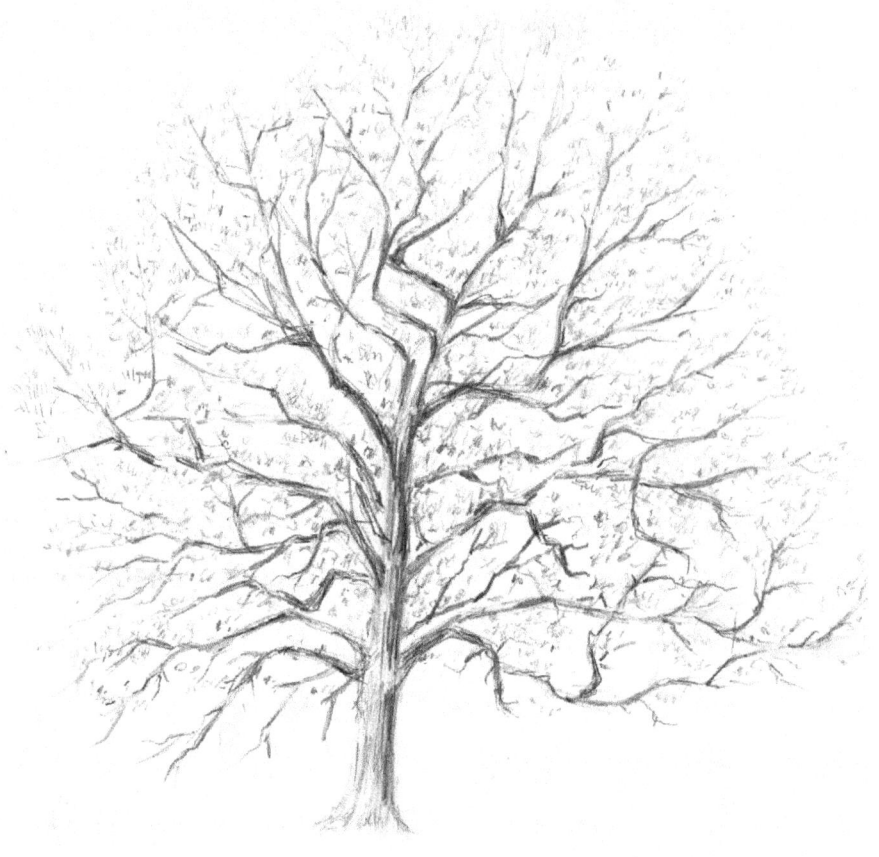

Finally the spring comes as the winter snows have melted away. Newly formed buds are seen on the branches as new life comes forth. It is a time of new beginnings and new growth. The sounds of birds are heard and the pastel hues are now being seen in their beauty. This maple tree will form beautiful green leaves in the summer and will be adorned with the nuances of violet, gold, orange, and alizarin as the autumn months finally come.

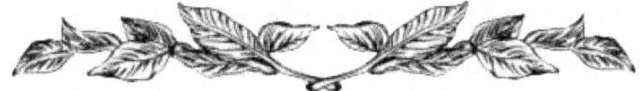

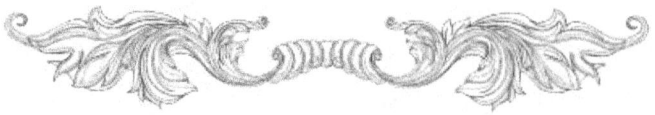

FACES IN TREES

Throughout the last several years I have incorporated hidden faces into the drawings of trees. I often see hidden images in the bark or limbs, as the light and shadows bring out various shapes and lines that somehow remind me of a face or a figure. Nature has a strange way of forming illusions in it, and sometimes a person's imagination gets the best of someone. But even with the beauty that is found in a tree, there are aspects of it at times that are metamorphosed into the semblance of other things. We all have a sense of imagination and a lot of this comes from nature.

Branches interlace each other and criss-cross forming patterns and designs. What one would see at first as mere branches and twigs can easily form the outline of a face or some other feature.

Where would we be in a world that is devoid of imagination, for without it everything becomes mundane and common place. We all perceive the world around us from our own viewpoints and perspectives. This is true of art and of many other walks of life.

While some of the drawings in this section may appear to be strange to some, allow your imagination to soar and perhaps you too, will begin to see the world around you in a different light.

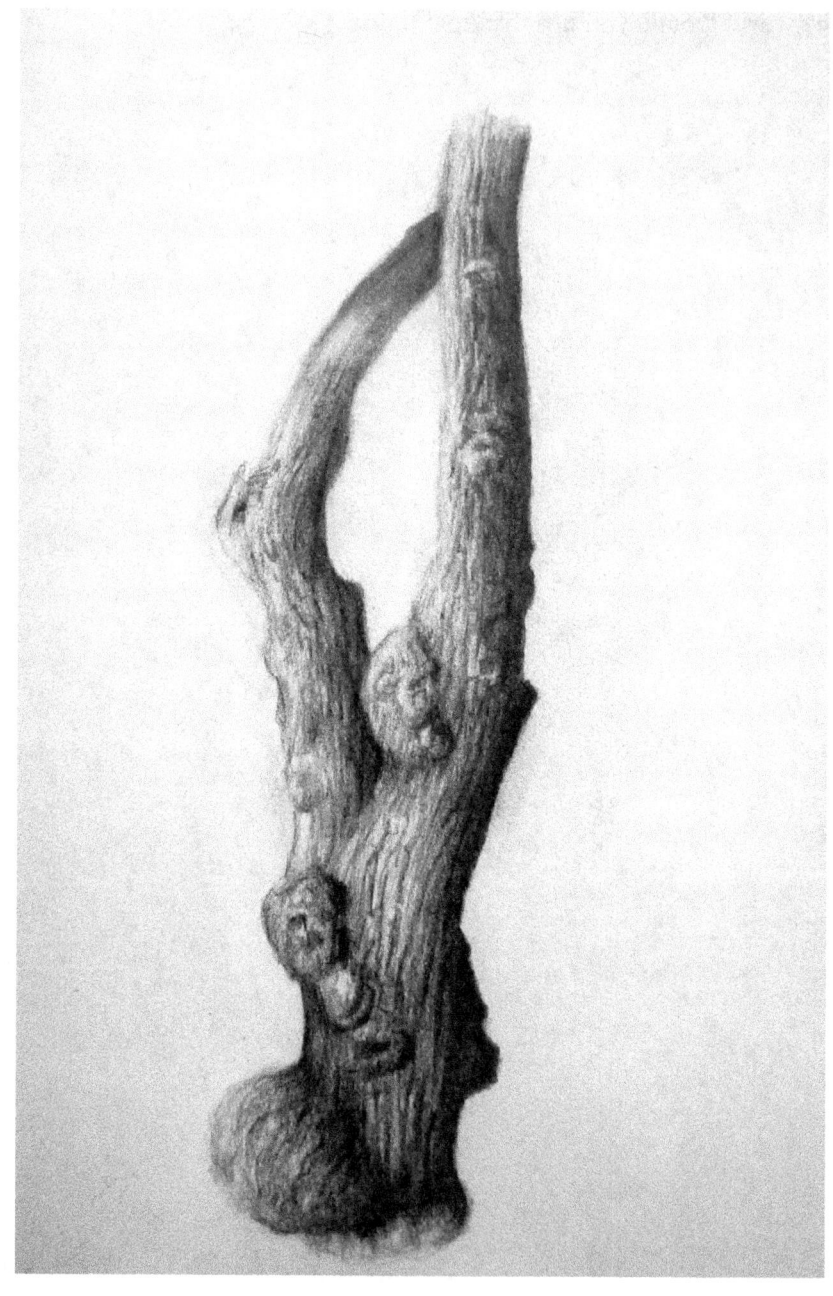

I saw this gnarled-looking tree at a camp area in Texas and as I kept drawing it, the knots on it seemed to take on the images of faces. It had unusual projections that emanated from the bark and trunk in certain sections of it. I don't know if this was due to some type of growth or what, but the tree certainly formed distinct areas on it that appeared to look like faces. The bulbous section at the base of the tree was also a strange thing to me as it seemed to create even more a sense of it being deformed. Nature has a way of creating unusual anomalies in it, and one can wonder how these things happen. But at any rate, it certainly allows one to appreciate the wide range of God's creation.

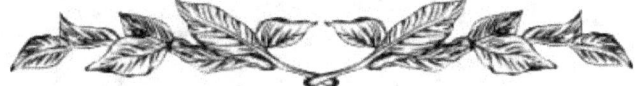

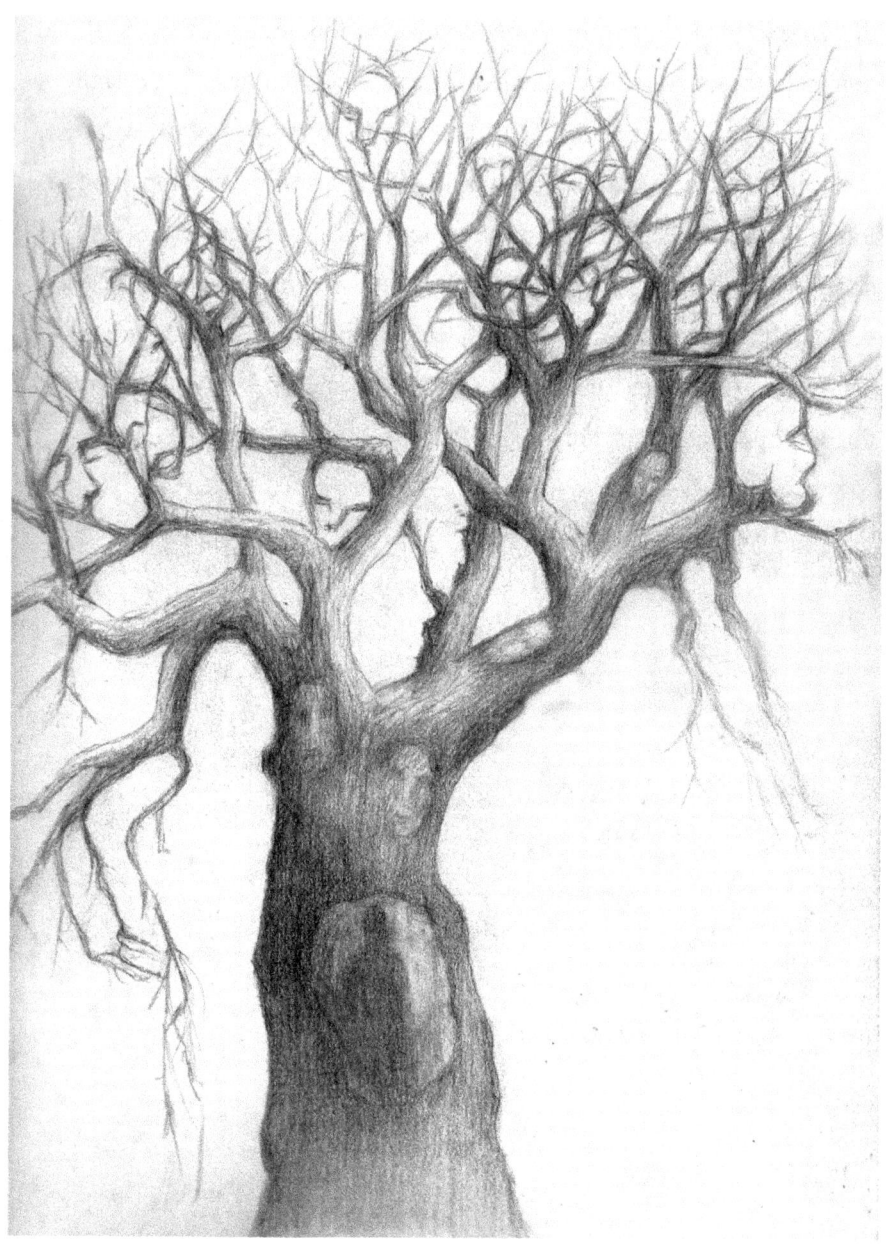

A few years ago I decided to do a drawing of a tree that had many faces in it. One can find some of these perhaps quite easily but then as you continue to look, you will see more. As I remember, there are close to thirty different images of faces to be seen in this tree. Remember to also consider where negative space is involved along a trunk or a branch. I had worked on this particular drawing when I was doing substitute teaching for the last few years. Many of the students enjoyed looking at it trying to find as many of the faces that they could.

Children are in many ways much more proficient at tapping into their imagination than most adults are. As we get older we are more constrained by the bills that we have to pay and the demands that are put on our lives, oftentimes prevent us from enjoying the simple pleasures of life that we enjoyed as a child.

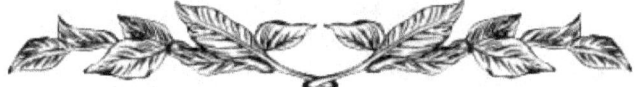

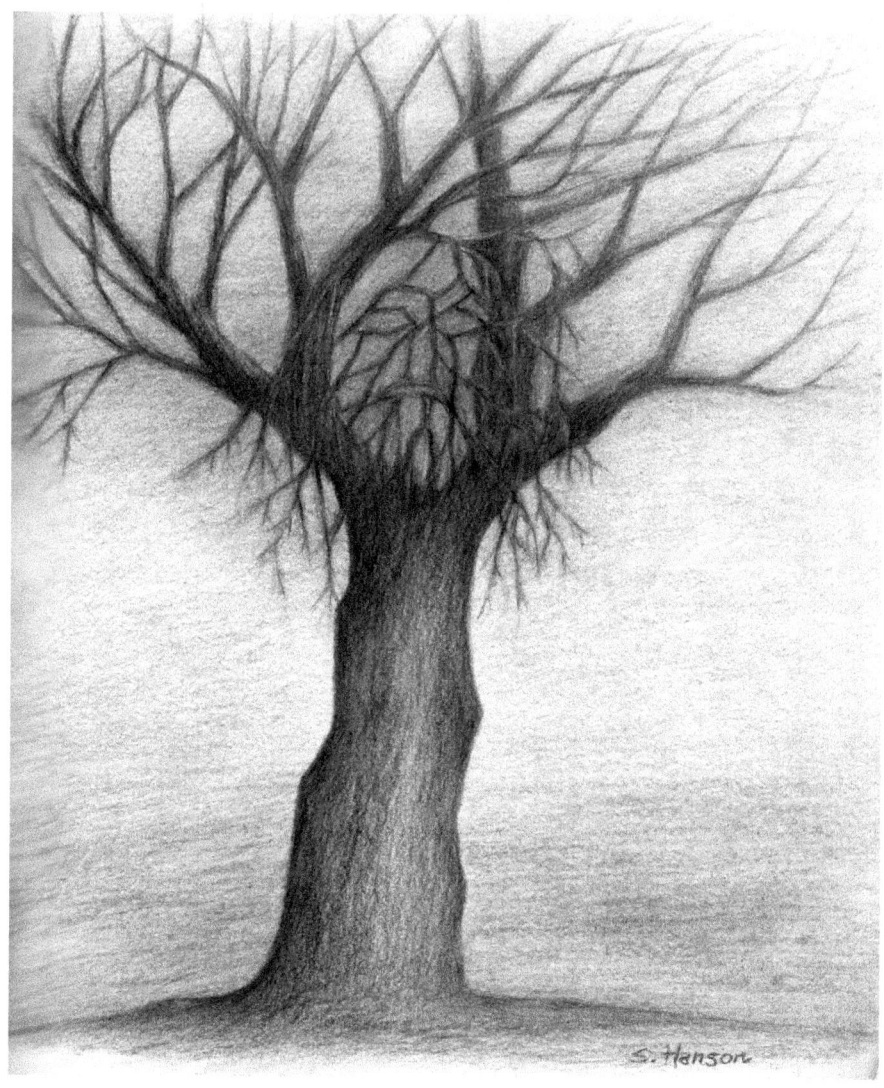

It is probably very obvious where the face is to be found in the previous drawing. This one is a simple demonstration of how branches and twigs can form a face.

As you take a walk today look at the trees around you and see if there are faces to be found within the interlacing branches. You may have to squint your eyes, but upon looking further, the image may come into view. It's not meant to be a thing to alarm or even frighten a person, but to just merely see things from a different point of view.

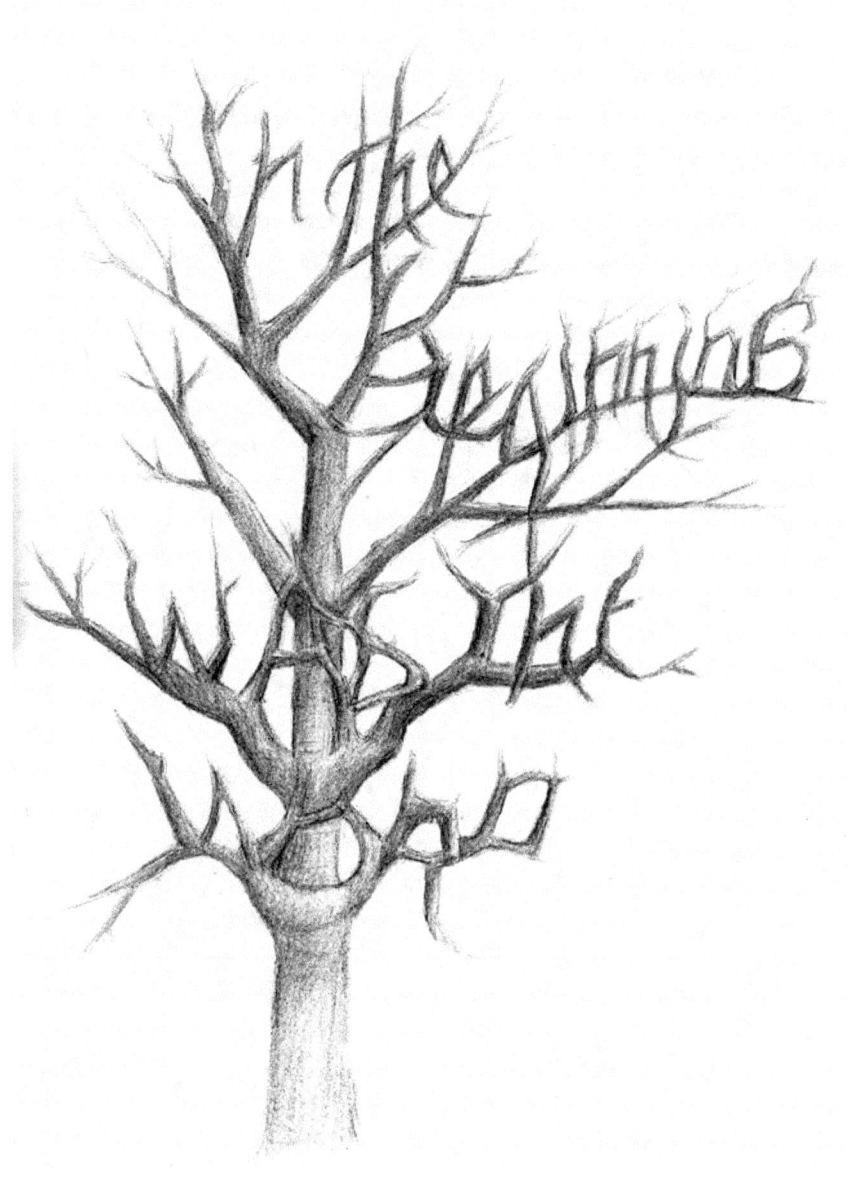

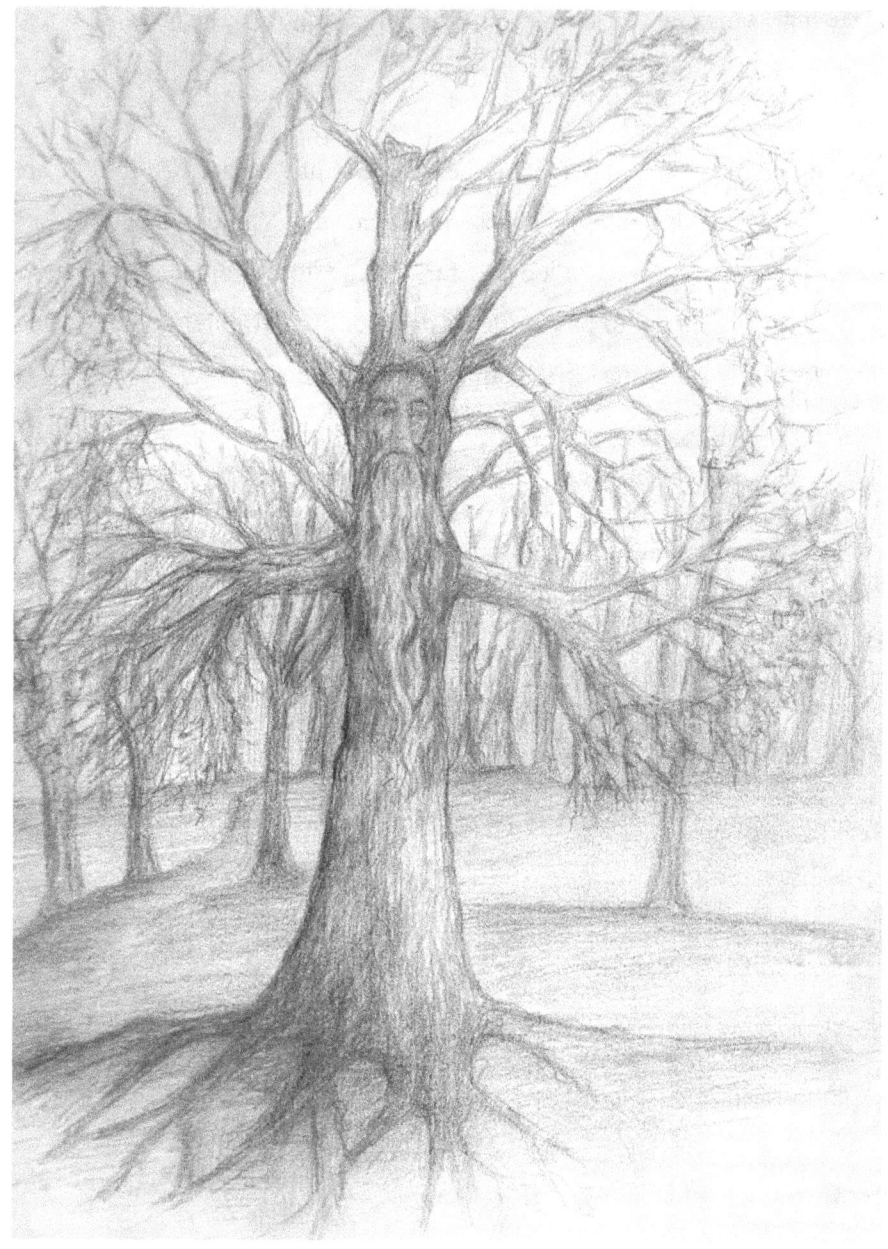

I wanted to depict an old bearded man in the previous drawing. Sometimes even the branches in a tree form appendages that look like arms or legs. Maybe this guy is the old man of the forest and he guards and protects it from danger. In Tolkien's classic, "Lord of the Rings," Fangorn Forest is guarded by Treebeard who is the leader of the Shepherds of the trees there.

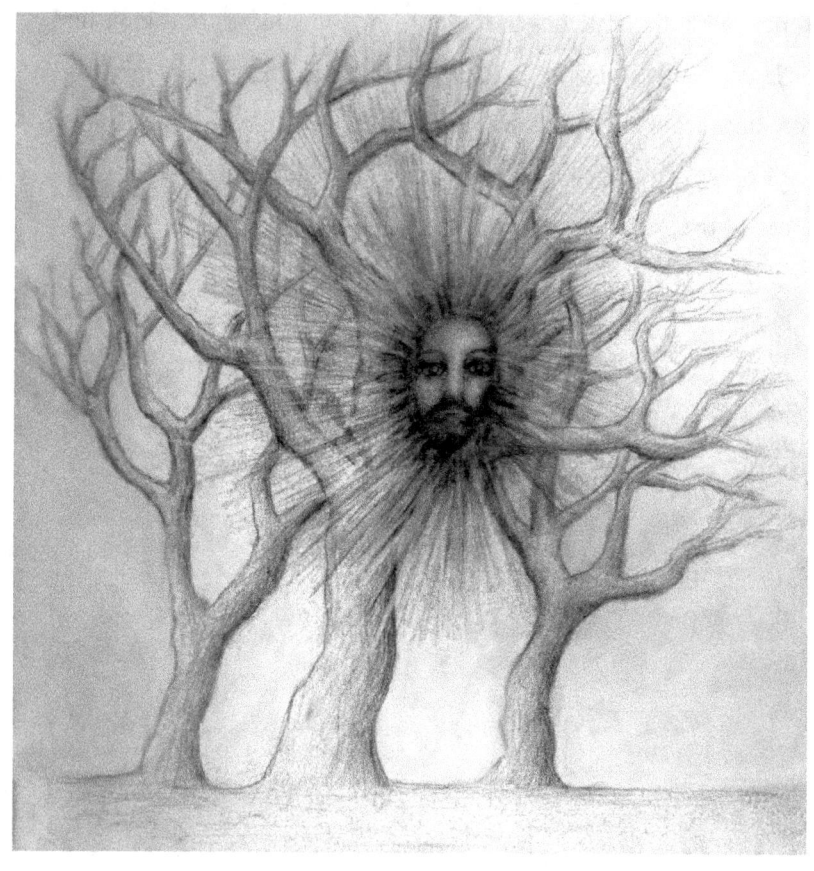

This drawing shows a face of Jesus shining forth throughout the branches. Certainly it would be very strange to see a sight like this and yet we know that the Lord Himself is very present around us. But sometimes we see a light permeating through the trees and one would know that this light dispels the darkness all around.

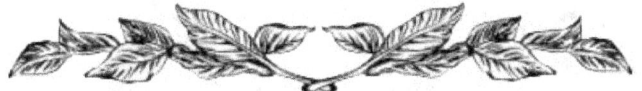

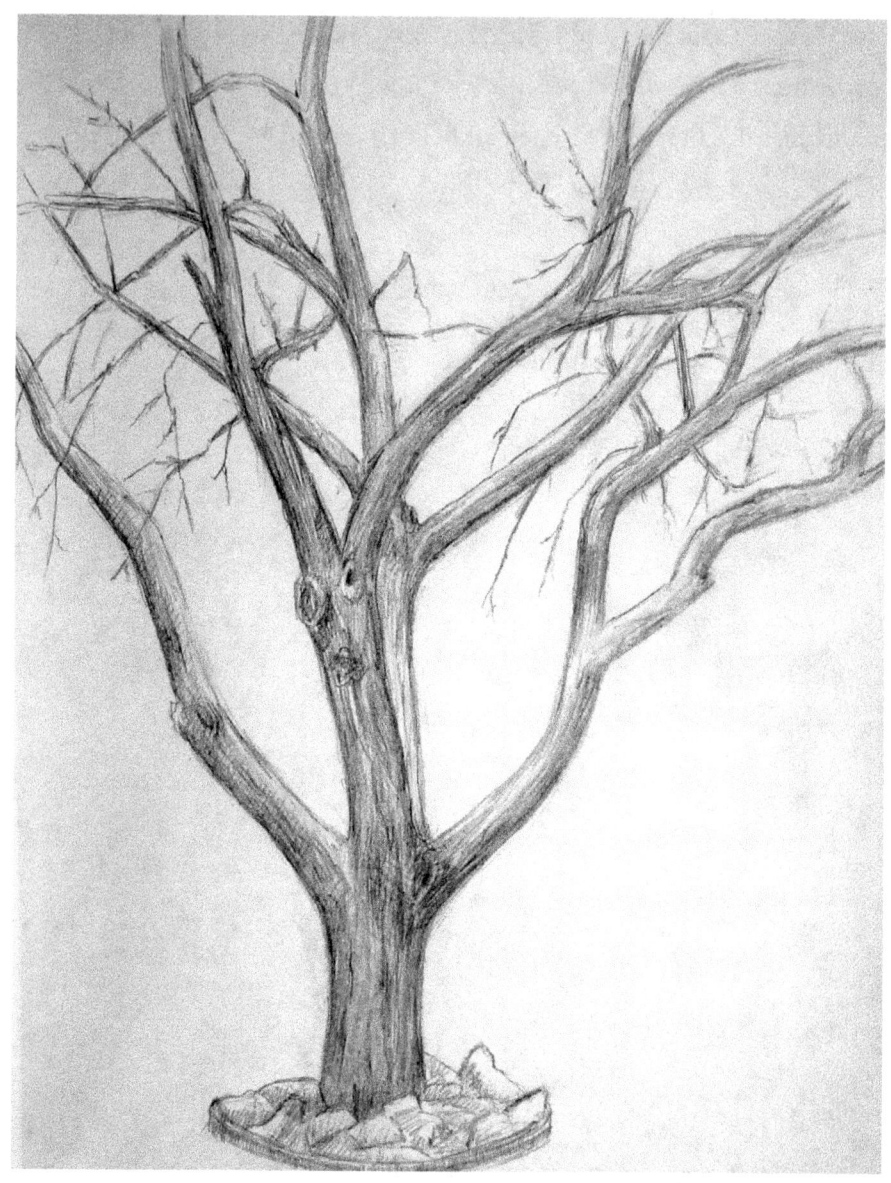

Several years ago we lived at a home where there was an interesting tree in the back yard. It usually had beautiful pink blossoms on it in the spring time but now all of the blossoms had long been gone. On one of the limbs was a strange anomaly and its appearance was very much like a type of face. This is how it looked.

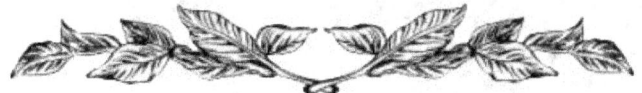

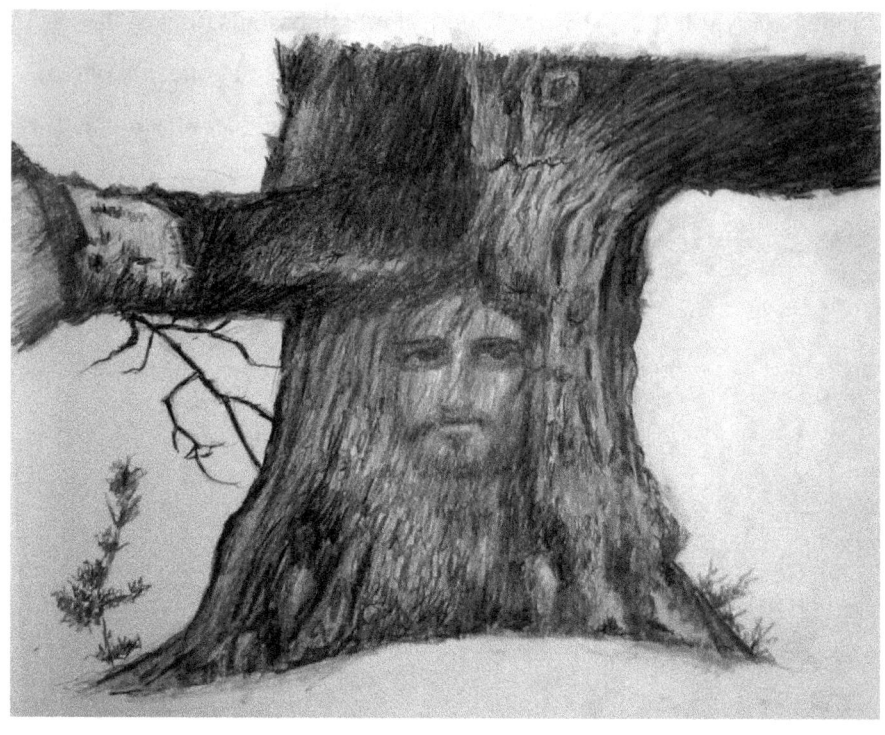

Many people see faces in trees and all types of surfaces. This face that is peering out within the bark of the tree could be something that one might see in the forest. The face can be readily seen in the texture of the bark in this tree as the eyes readily follow you. As you take a walk among the trees look around you and see what there is to be found; you might be surprised.

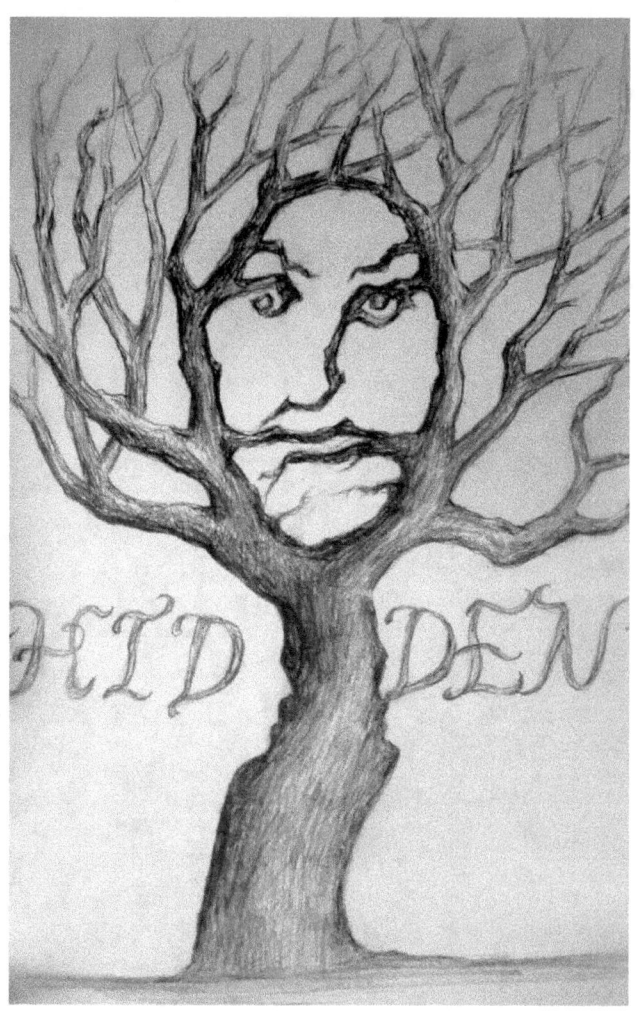

The drawing says HIDDEN and yet the image certainly isn't hidden. It is readily seen. The branches and the twigs form lips, eyes, and a mouth. The features of a face can be manipulated and formed as each twig is bent and overlaps another one. Oftentimes faces and objects are formed naturally in a tree, but the artist can do what he or she wants to do in order to create the image desired.

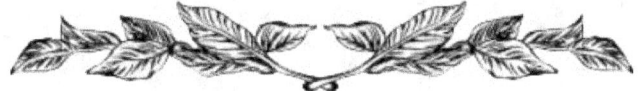

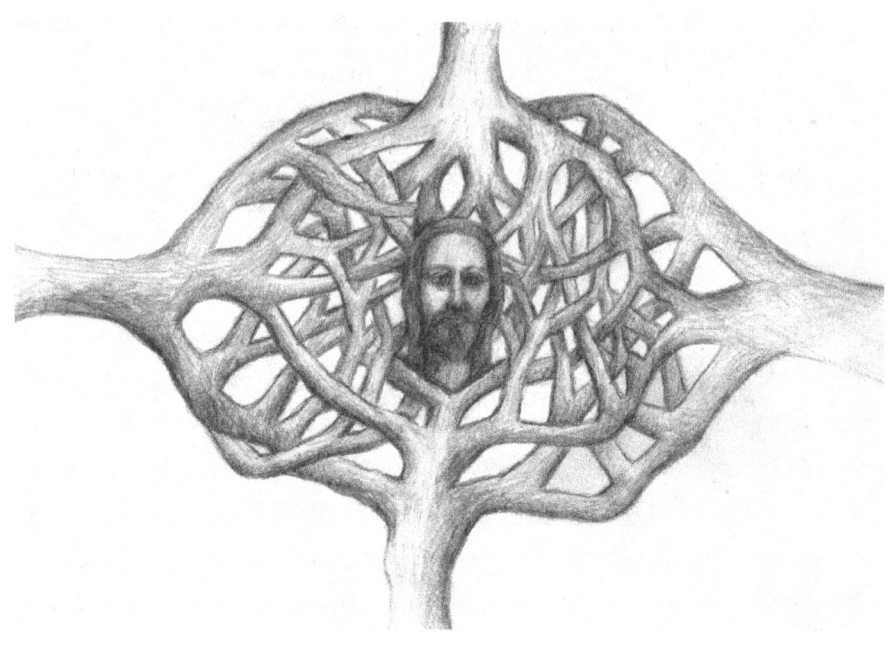

Designs can be formed as branches overlap and intersect each other. One can see these types of patterns in the roots of trees particularly as their limbs form a lacey picture. In the midst of designs that are formed there is usually an open space within the center. Here again I decided to depict the image of a face that we well know. The roots of a tree are as detailed as the limbs and branches are and they must be considered as a part of the whole assembly.

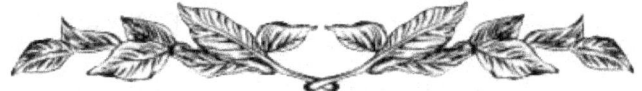

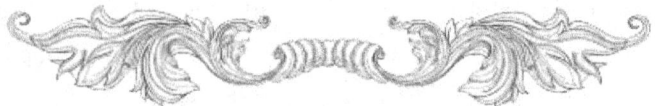

TREES WITH WORDS

As branches and twigs interlace and overlap themselves, sometimes words can be seen. There can be simple words that can be formed or sometimes a complete phrase or sentence. But whatever the word or phrase that is chosen, one needs to figure out how to incorporate it into the branches and overall look of a tree.

This section displays several examples I have done using words that are drawn into and around the branches. Words and letters can be hidden or in some cases, they become much more obvious to the viewer.

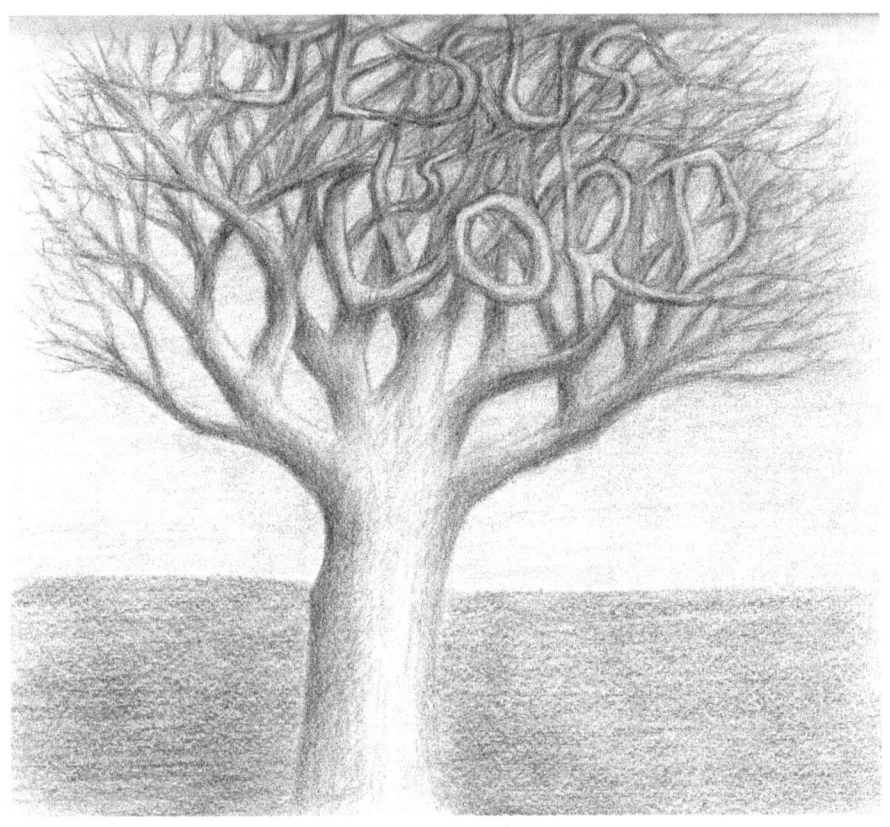

As I had said, simple words and phrases can be drawn and manipulated as branches are formed. As I begin the drawing of a tree I see how a letter or a word can be inserted. . It's a process of going back and forth between the images and eventually the word is formed. In this case, the phrase, "Jesus is Lord" has been drawn into the image of the tree. While the phrase is easily seen and identified, one could certainly make it look much more hidden.

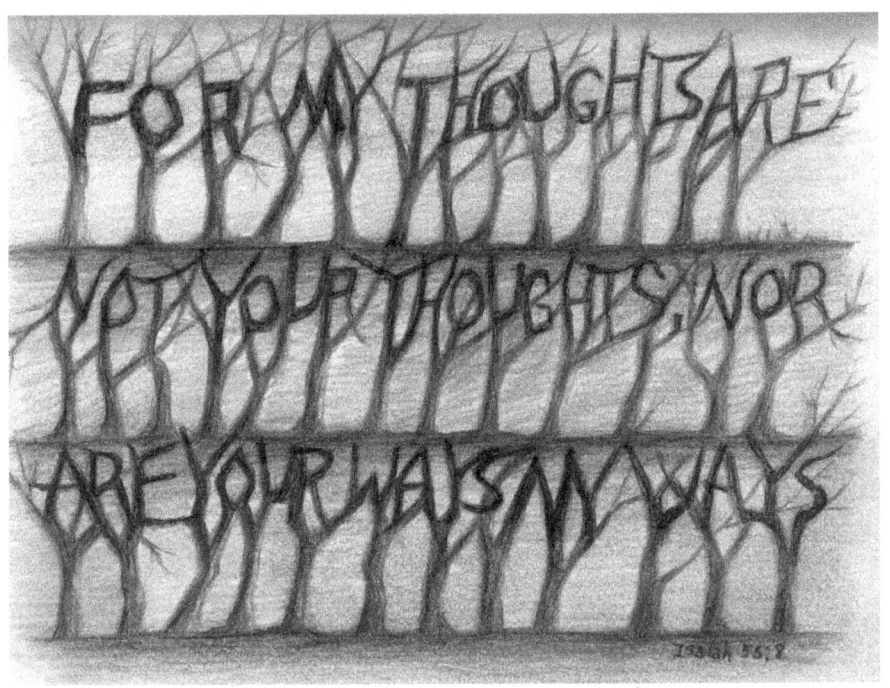

I decided to form rows of trees for this particular drawing because the words wouldn't fit within just a few of them. Typically trees grow randomly but occasionally they are seen in rows forming hedge trees and along roads. This time I chose to have three rows of trees to create the phrases that are here. For as we know our thoughts are not the thoughts of God, for His ways are much higher than ours.

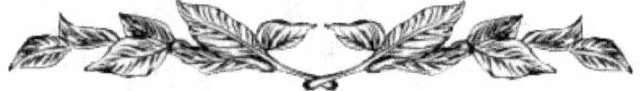

There are as many different types of trees as there are people. The sharp pointed limbs of this particular type of tree seemed to be suitable for the formation of words going out to the branches. The words here seem to take on the very look of wood and texture. There is a wooden quality to them, and yet even so, the words are alive because they are formed in the word of God.

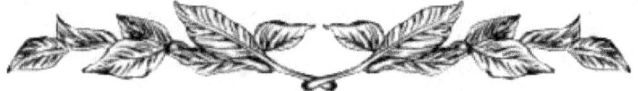

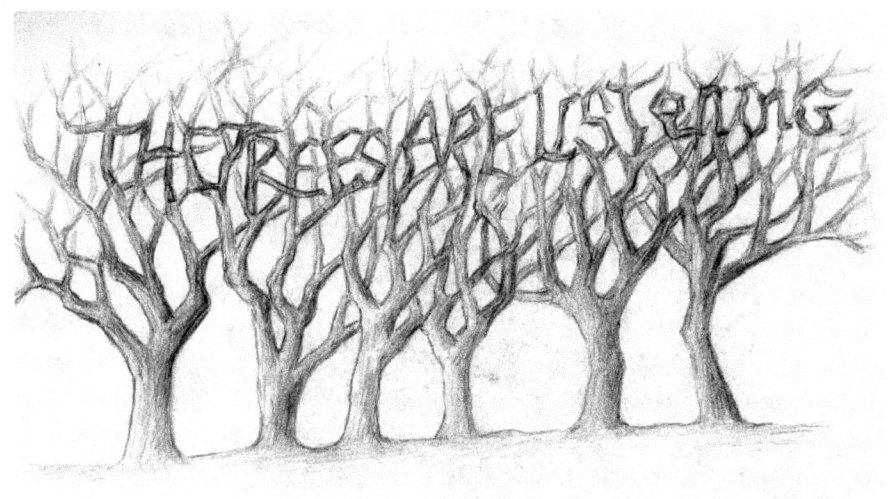

When one is out in nature it can seem very much like you are in the presence of God. One can also sense that they are being watched and that you are not alone. I'm not referring to a sense of paranoia or of feeling afraid but merely that even the very trees are listening. One can certainly imagine how many people have walked amidst the trees that we see, and over the years I'm sure that they would have quite a story to tell.

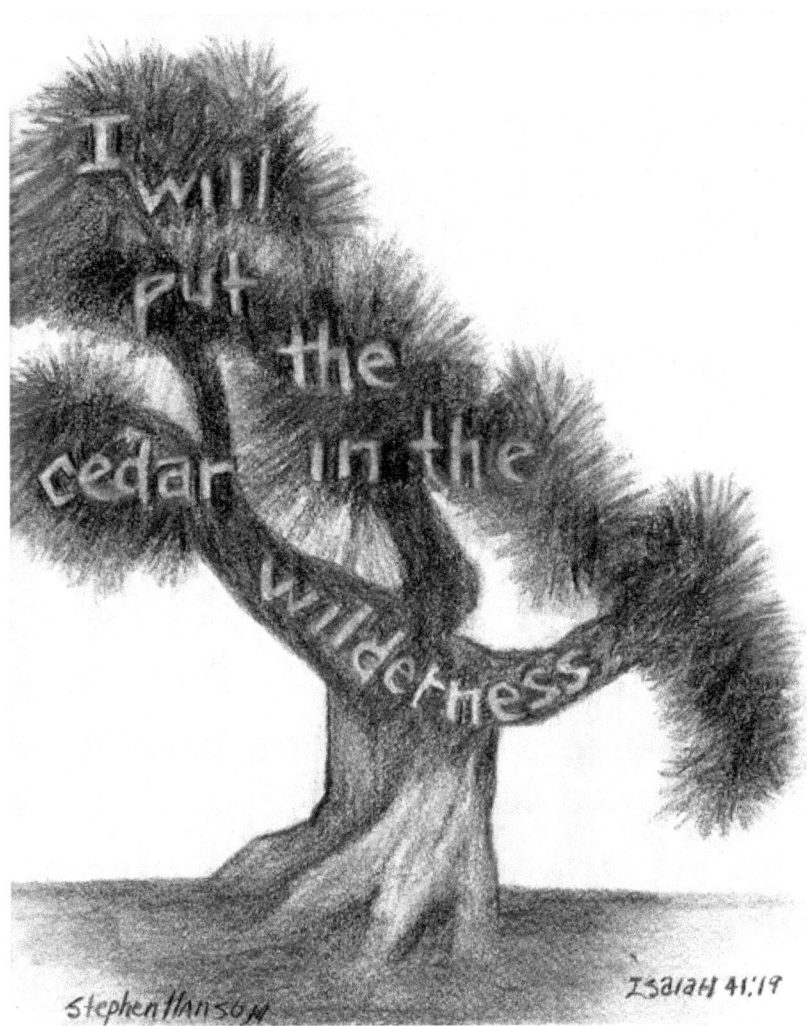

Cedar trees are different from other evergreen trees. They have a rather coarse appearance and texture especially to the touch. But they are a strong and hearty type of tree that oftentimes grows higher up in the mountains. The winds can blow at it and yet it remains steady and endures throughout the years. God has said that He has put the cedar in the wilderness.

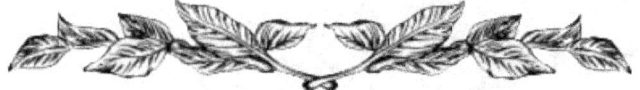

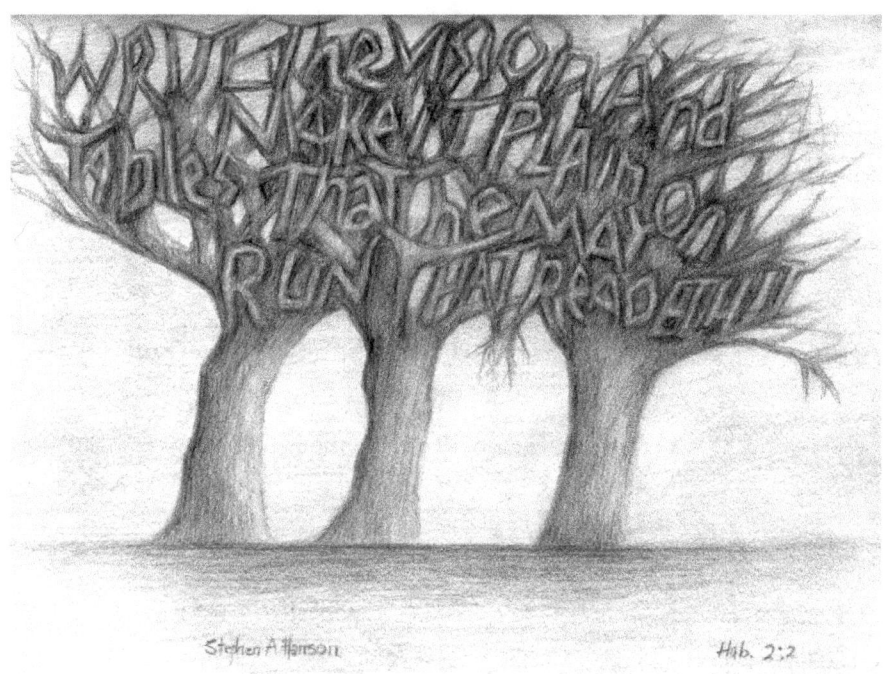

Words are important and we see them inscribed into the pages of books and they serve to remind us of what is important to us. Words have also been chiseled into stone markers in graveyards to mark the lives and memories of the ones who have lived in this world.

We are told that the vision is written down on tablets so that one would run with the message. The vision may wait a long time before it is realized but if we are patient, we will see it come.

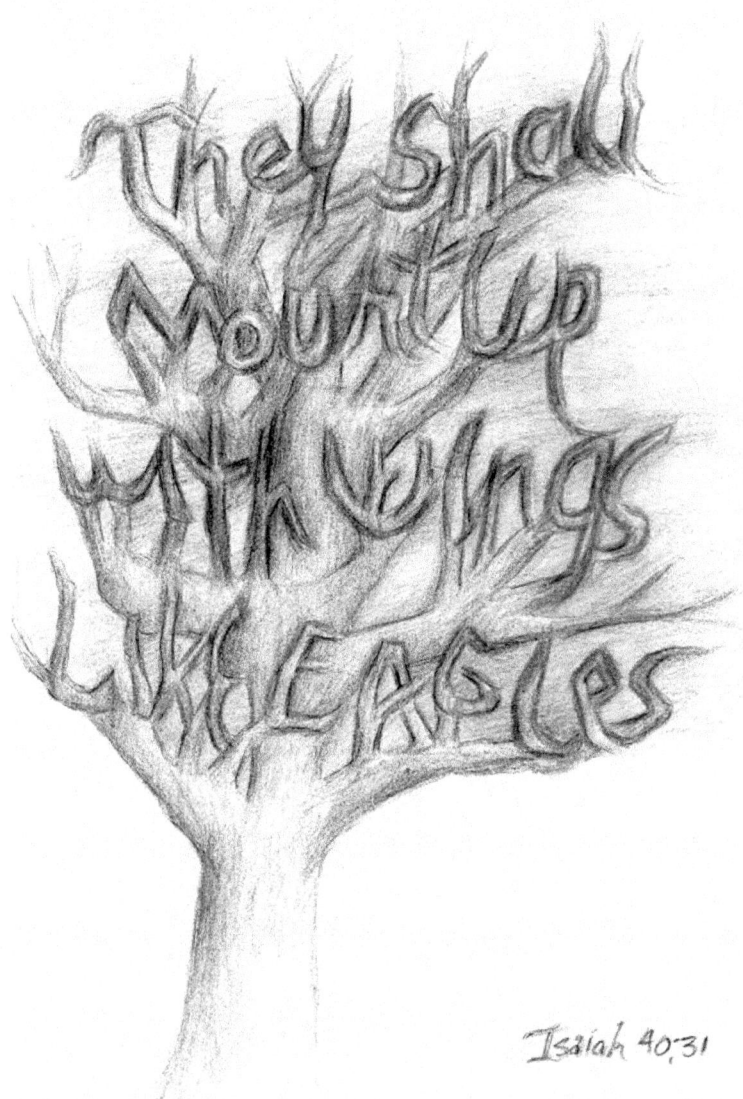

Isaiah 40:31

Words can lift us up or they can bring us down. Words are powerful and they can have a lasting effect upon us. The eagles build nests high up in the cliffs so that they are protected from predators. And yet even we can mount-up with wings as of eagles as we wait upon the Lord to renew our strength.

[31] But they that wait upon the LORD shall renew their strength; they shall mount up with wings as eagles; they shall run, and not be weary; and they shall walk, and not faint. Isaiah 40

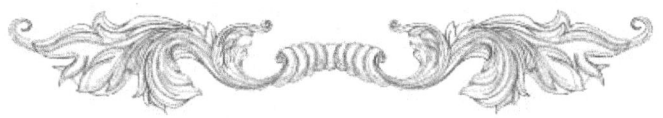

LANDSCAPE WITH TREES

Typically a landscape painting is one in which there are many trees that are seen among the hills, mountains, or streams. There is a unity to be found as the various elements relate to each other. One gives predominance to different things in a landscape so that a point of interest is formed. Otherwise, all of the details have equal value and one can easily lose focus of what is important.

Just as one would create a landscape painting so also a person can do a drawing of it. In this section that is what I have chosen to do as various trees form the scenery.

Some of these drawings have been used to create paintings while others have been left as a complete thing unto themselves.

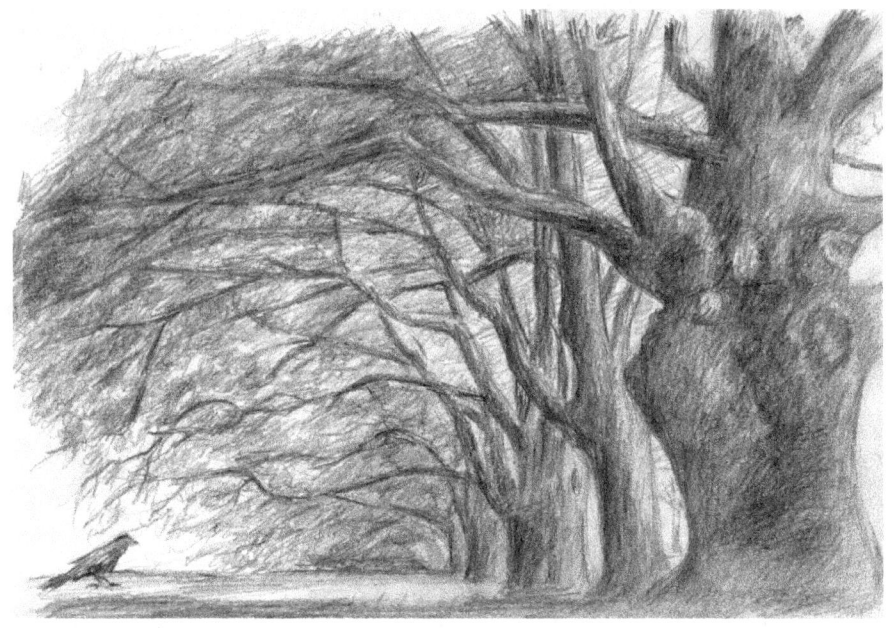

This was a grove of willow trees and it seemed to be a good place to include a raven beside them. The bird is a sentinel as it sits on the parameter waiting and watching for whatever might come. Ravens are very smart birds and probably are the most intelligent to be found in the world. Even though they are scavengers they alert other animals to feed and find sustenance.

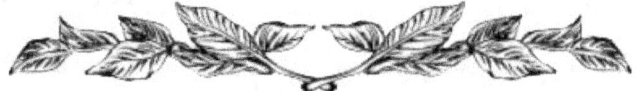

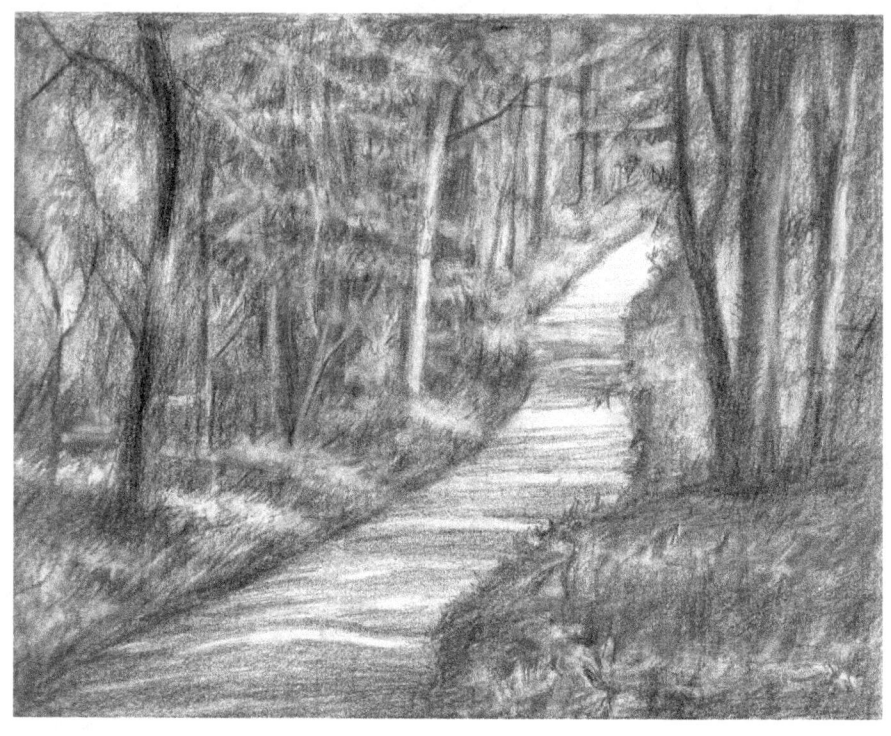

Pathways signify many things and they have always served as a source of inspiration to me. This one winds its way through the trees and goes back into the distance further out of view. I also did a painting from this particular drawing. There were a myriad of different types of greens and earthen tones that I used to do the painting. One can't see the colors in this drawing, but perhaps the various tones can give the appearance that I was striving to get.

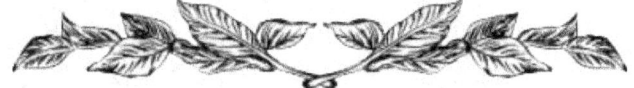

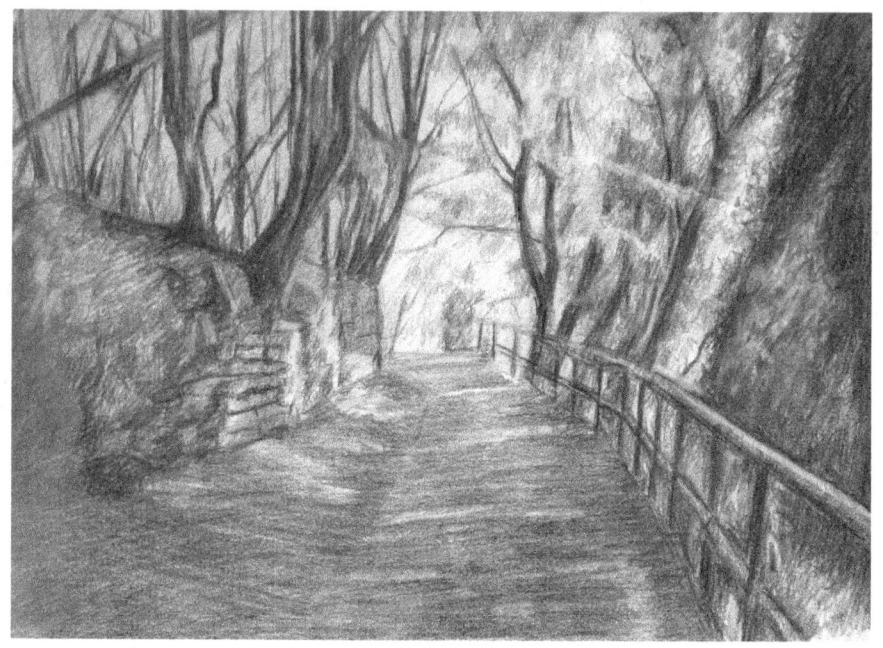

Again this drawing has a path winding its way beside some trees. I enjoyed doing this particular one also because of the light and shadows that fell upon the road. While a painting of this subject matter would depict the colors and tones in it much more proficiently, the silvery areas achieved through pencil can give one the feeling of a scene in its entirety.

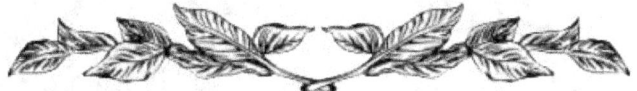

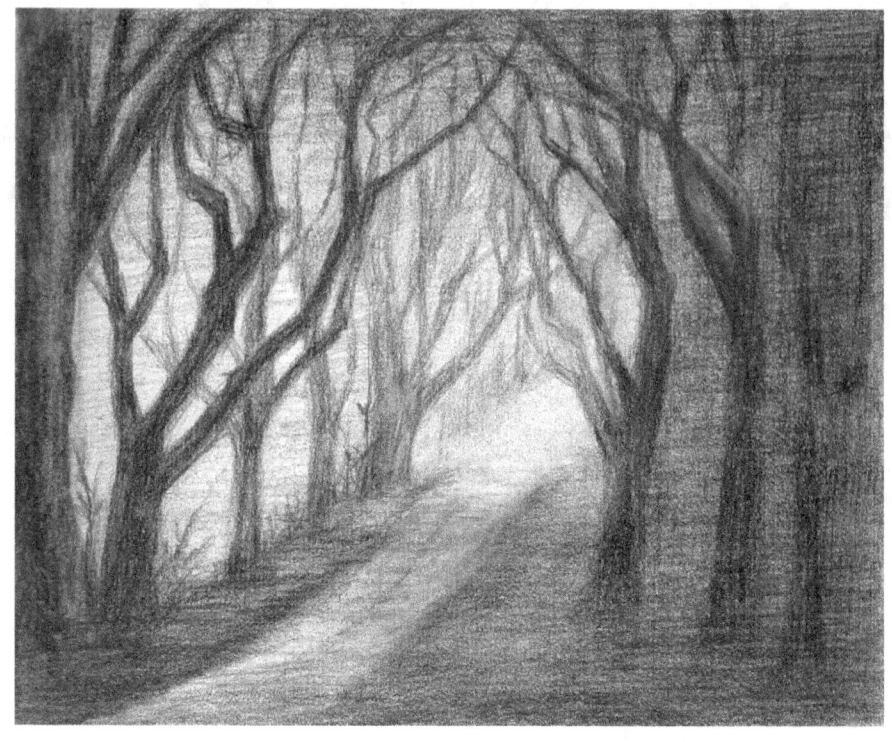

This particular drawing was to emphasize the sense of a light that was seen deep in the forest at the end of a pathway that led into it. The light spreads forth and permeates throughout the trees providing a sense of hope and warmth to all who might enter in. I did a painting from this drawing and it is available on my website.

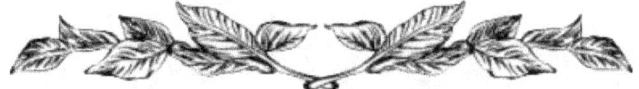

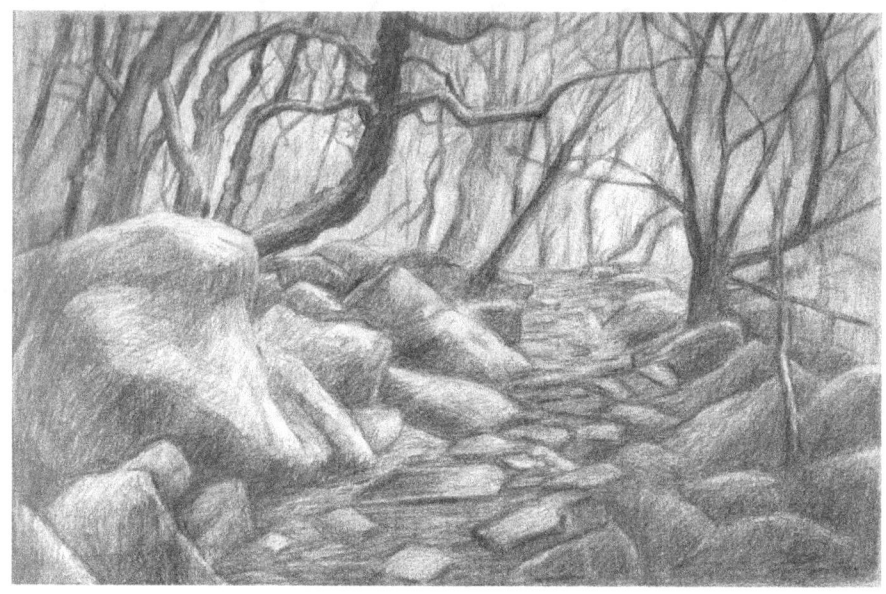

Now this drawing leads one along the rocks over a river bed instead of a pathway through the forest. I've always enjoyed drawing and painting rocks for they signify a sense of strength and endurance. This entire place was filled with rocks and stones of all kinds of sizes and shapes. One could carefully walk upon the stones as it wound its way upwards through the wooded area.

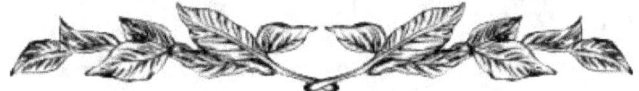

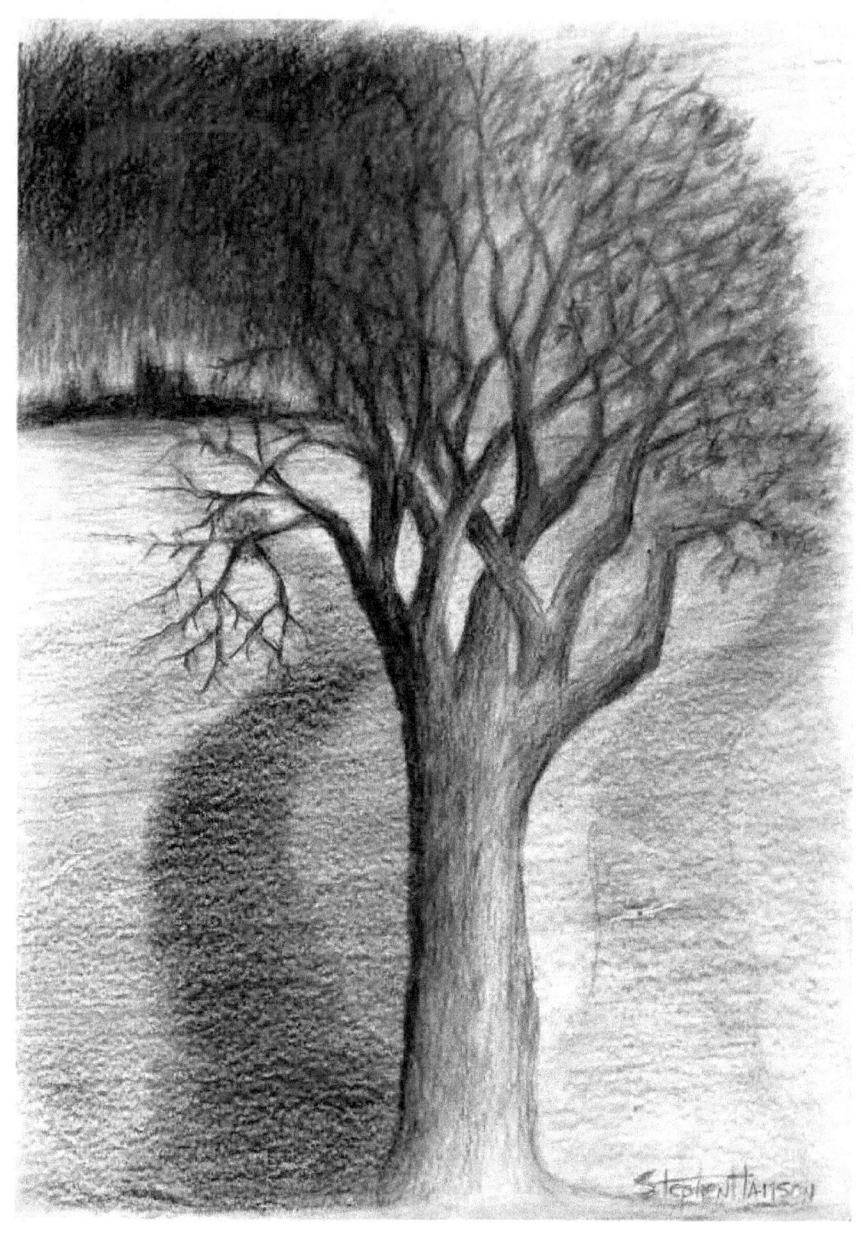

This previous drawing is very symbolic in nature as it represents two paths that one might choose to take in this life. So of course, one side of the drawing would be in darkness and the one in light. Even the tree itself has half of it bathed in light while the other side is enclosed in darkness. The decisions that we choose to take in this life will lead us along either one of these pathways. We must choose wisely.

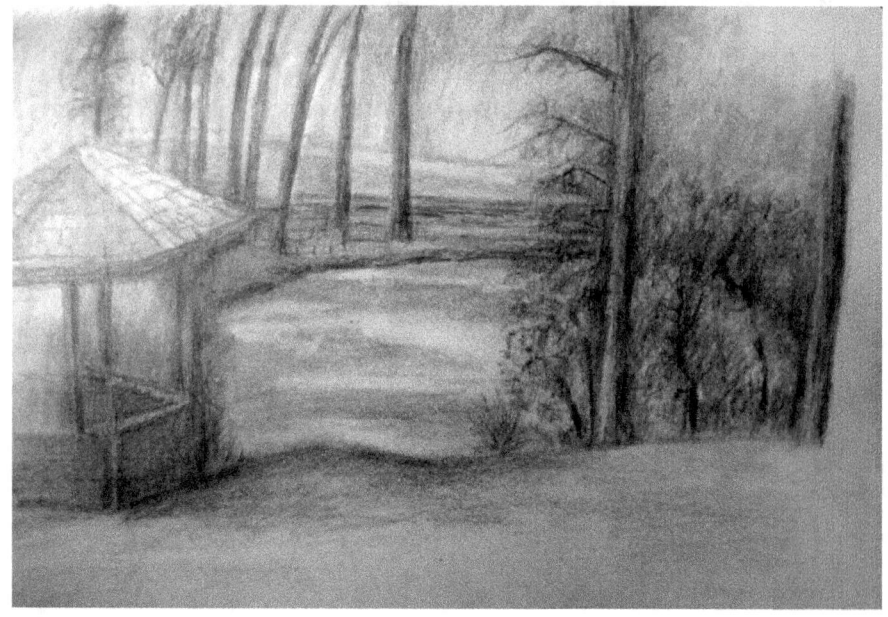

I sat down and drew this little drawing a couple of months ago while we stayed at Colorado Heights RV Park. This little gazebo was right beside a pond where people can fish or just sit and relax. It's a beautiful place to stay for a while and we have enjoyed being here off-and-on during the warmer months. It's also close by so that we can visit family and friends. There are large, majestic Ponderosa Pine trees all around and various activities that one can join in and partake of.

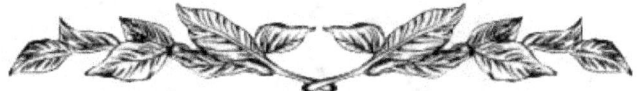

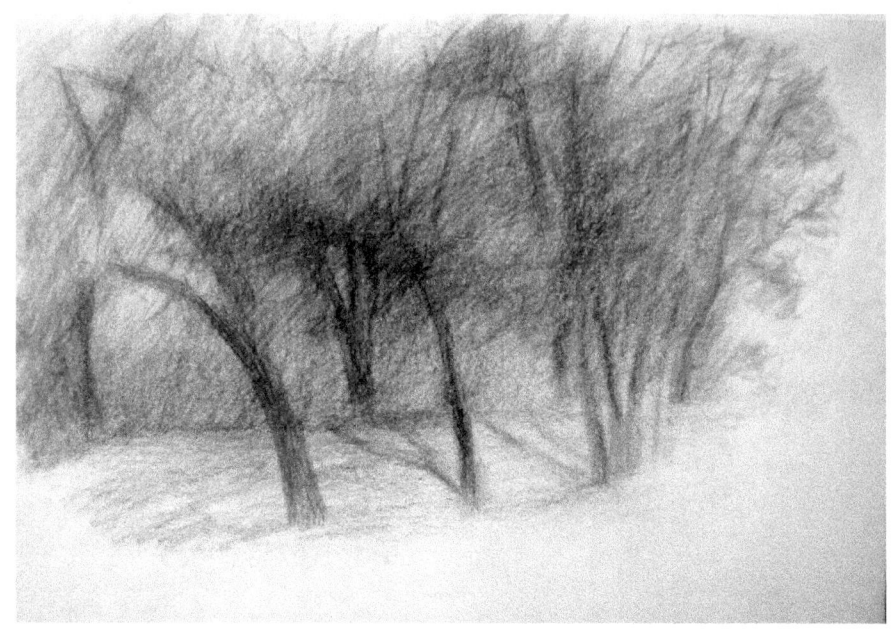

This is a simple little sketch of some trees that I found when we were camping this past summer up in the mountains west of Colorado Springs. There is so much to see in nature and one needs to make decisions quickly as to what to use and what to discard in a drawing. Sometimes simplicity is the key. There is so much else I could have added in this drawing but I decided to give it a softer appearance.

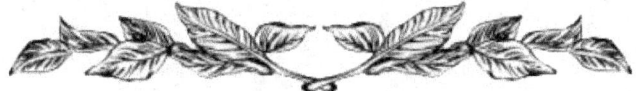

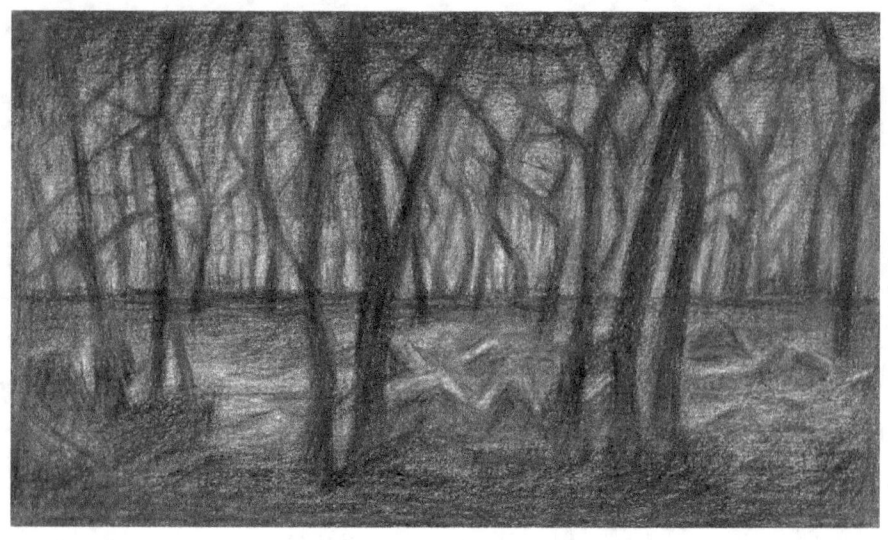

In the deep of the forest there is a sense of mystery and awe. One can't quite put a finger on it, but if one visits there often soon enough they may well be transported back to olden times and think about storybook characters and settings. The original drawing has deep browns, greens, and purples in it, but of course I couldn't include it because this book is just devoted to black and white examples.

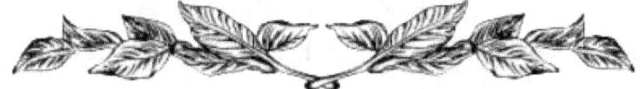

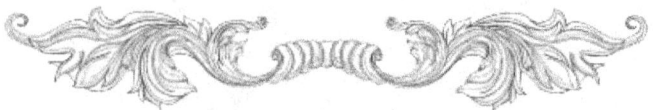

TREES WITH PEOPLE

Sometimes adding the other element of a figure in a drawing adds something needed to it. People are part of the landscape and even though one goes out into the wild to get away from them, we still share in the process. In the past I've done a few drawings from biblical scenes and these incorporate a tree or something from a landscape in them.

It can be challenging to know how to create the right sense of proportion and perspective when adding people to a landscape drawing or painting. It of course also depends upon what one wants to emphasize in the work. Either the figure can take predominance or it can be something secondary to the landscape itself.

One can see many examples from the Old Masters when they incorporated figures into a landscape in their paintings. Although the ones I've done here are quite simple and in no way have the complexity or beauty that is found in the works of the Old Masters.

This is just another avenue of expression that I have decided to do in this little book.

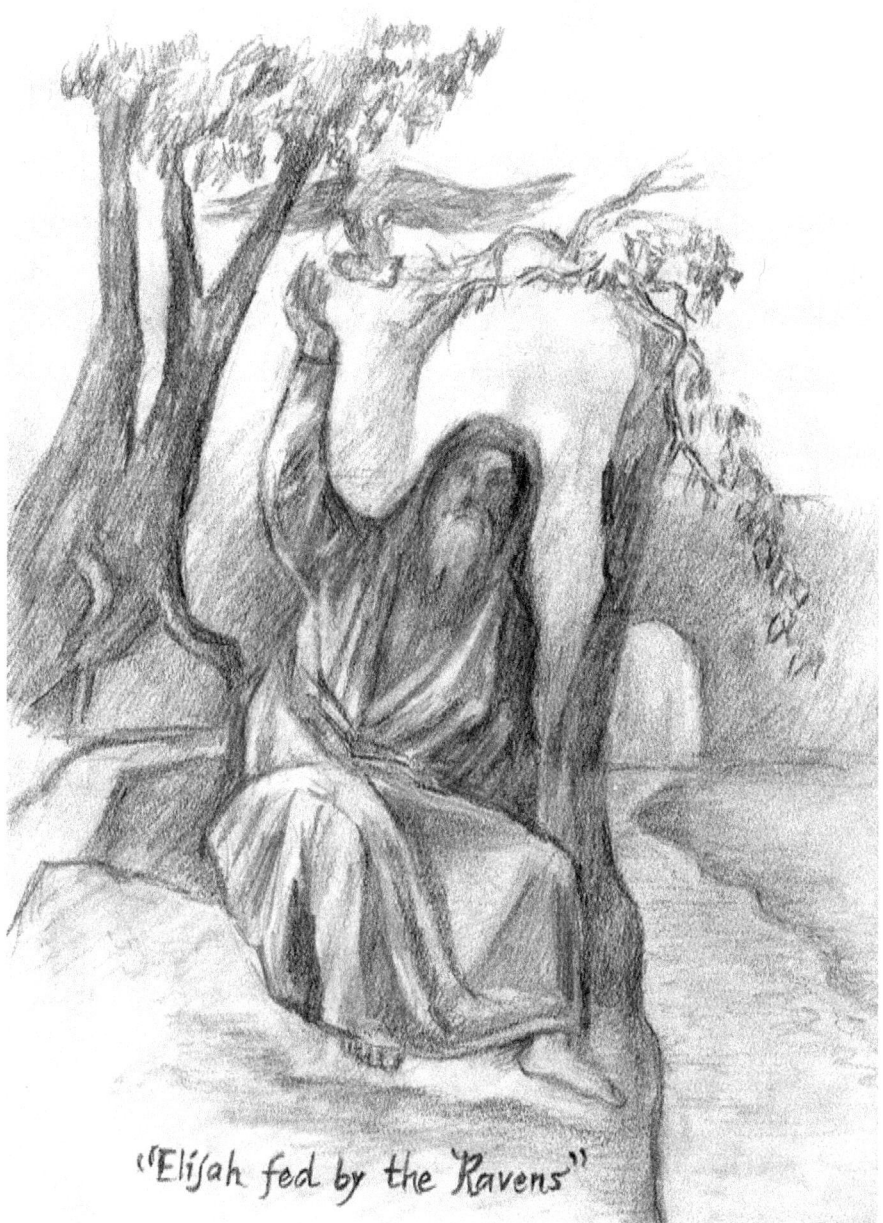

"Elijah fed by the Ravens"

The prophet Elijah was fed in the wilderness by ravens. It was a miraculous thing as they brought him sustenance. In the past I used to do paintings of ravens and I included them frequently when I did paintings of a southwestern theme. We don't know exactly what the terrain may have looked like as the prophet stayed by the brook, but there was food and water for him there sent from the Lord Himself.

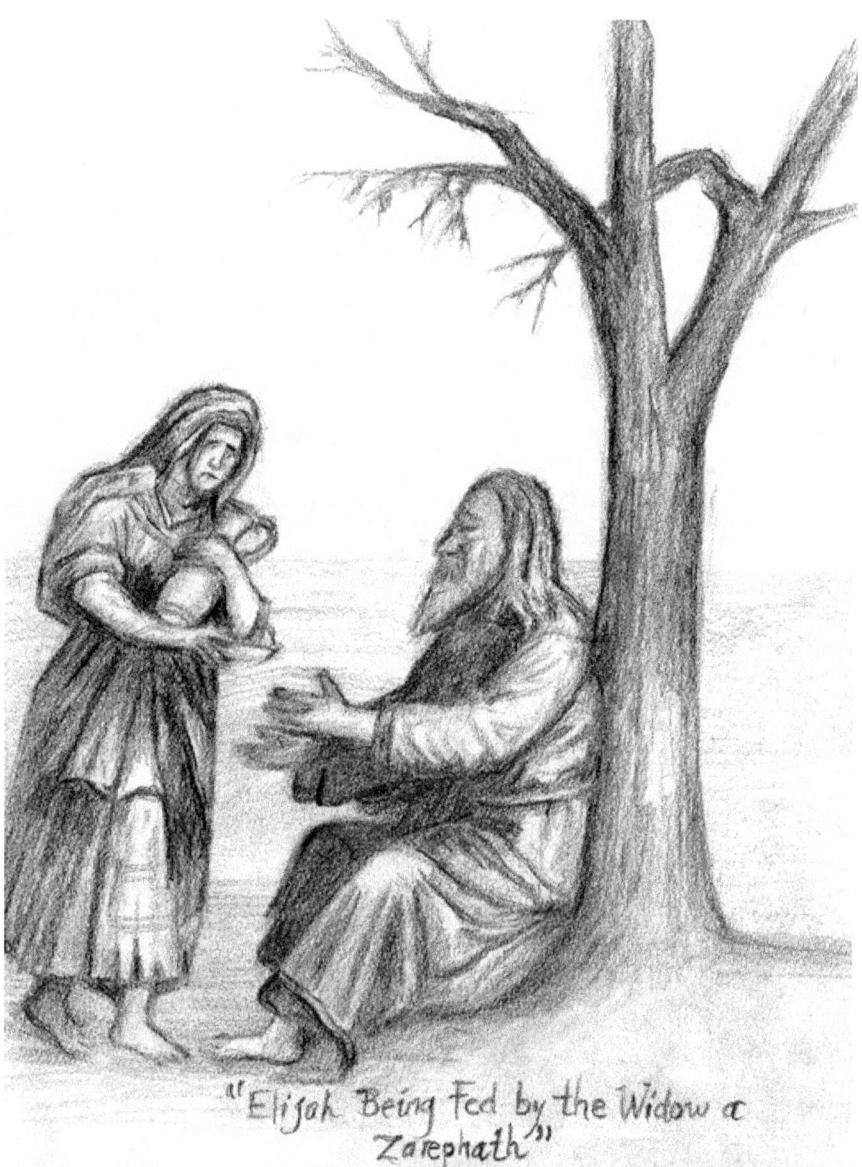

"Elijah Being Fed by the Widow a Zarephath"

This time the prophet was given sustenance through the widow at Zarephath. She had run out of oil and flour but because she believed in the word of the Lord, she along with the prophet and her son, were fed for a long time. So, because trees are found almost anywhere, I thought that this was a good place to have one as it provided shade from the sun for the widow and the prophet.

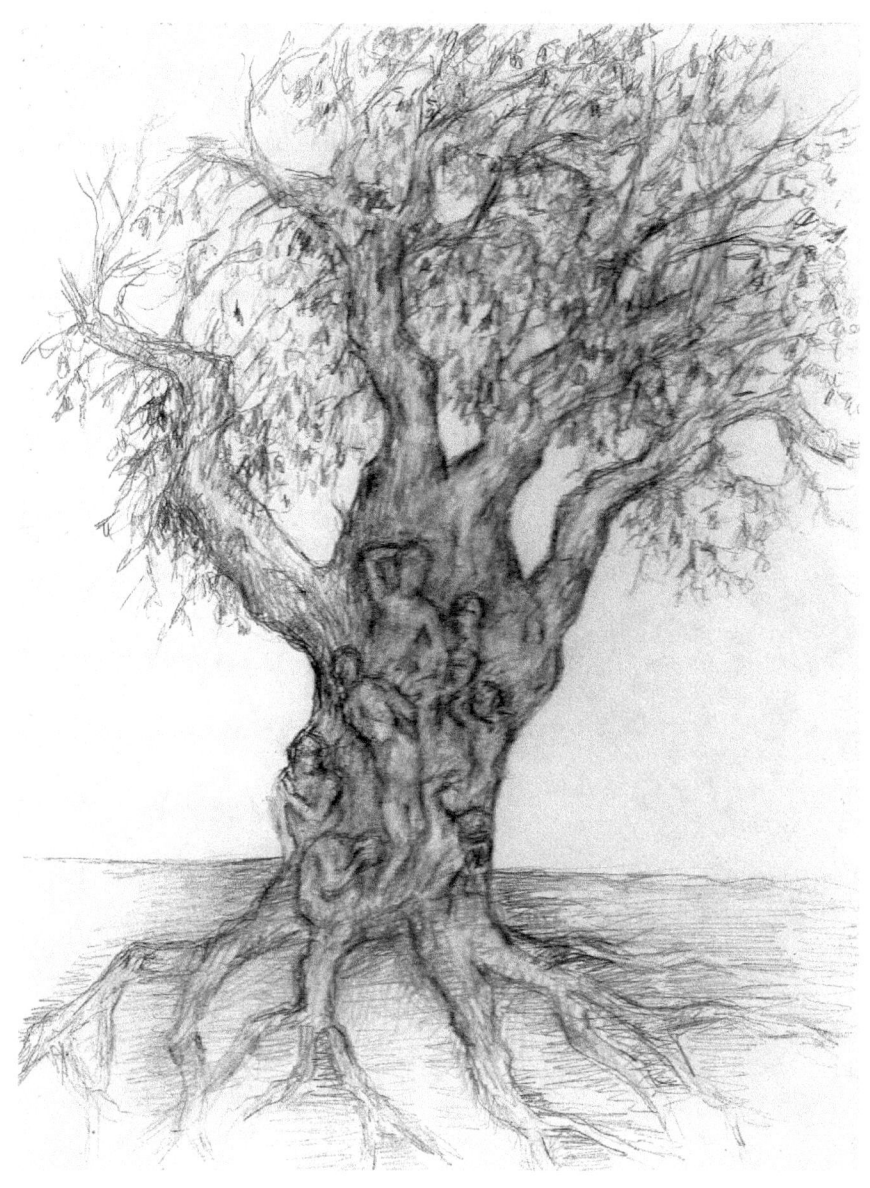

The tree of life is a well-known theme and it has been used creatively by many artists over the years. I wanted to do a drawing of people within a tree that would show that there is "life" within this tree pulsating and giving a place for people as they dwell within and rise up through its branches. That's not to say that we are given life through a tree or anything else in nature, but that the tree of life is of course a spiritual thing as we are identified with Christ. The artist though, chooses his own avenues of expression to show this theme.

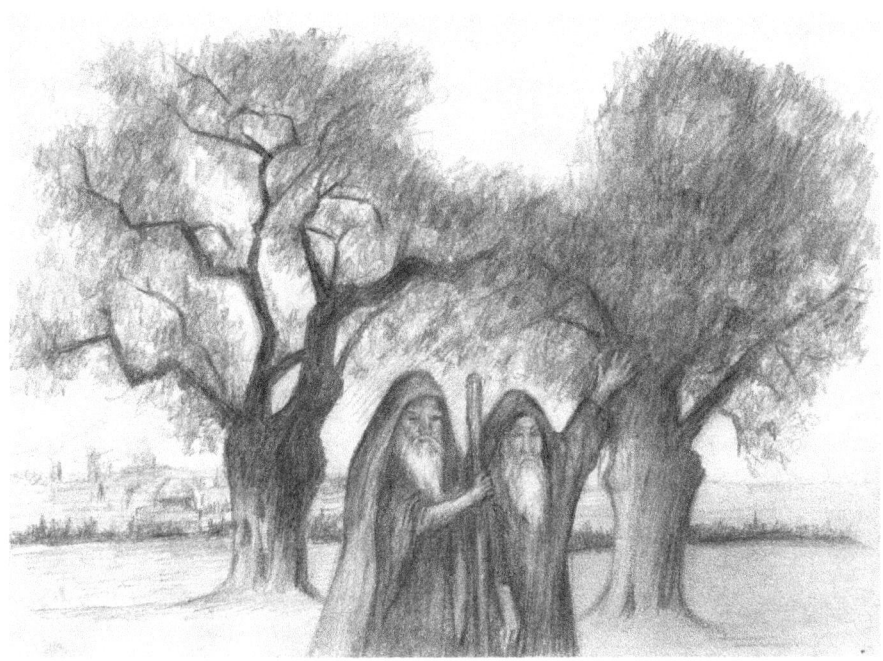

This drawing identifies the two witnesses as described in the bible at the end of the age in the book of Revelation. They are described as the two olive trees, and so I thought it good to draw a couple of large olive trees behind them.

The Two Witnesses

11 *Then there was given me a measuring rod like a staff; and someone said, "Get up and measure the [1]temple of God and the altar, and those who worship in it. [2] Leave out the court which is outside the temple and do not measure it, for it has been given to the nations; and they will tread under foot the holy city for forty-two months. [3] And I will grant authority to my two witnesses, and they will prophesy for twelve hundred and sixty days, clothed in sackcloth." [4] These are the two olive trees and the two lampstands that stand before the Lord of the earth. Rev. 11*

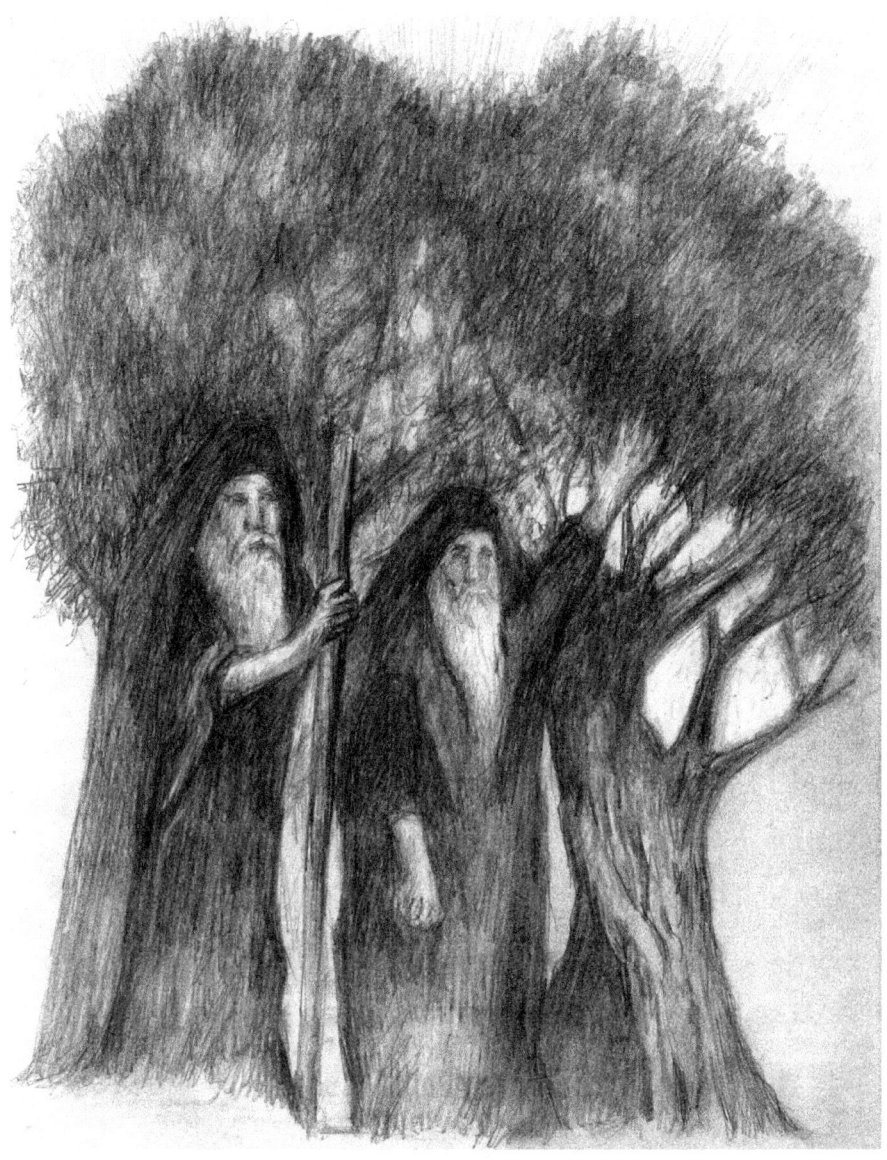

This is another rendition of the same theme from the previous page of the two witnesses. I wanted to do a closer view of the figures as they stood in front of the two olive trees. Sometimes the artist needs to do more than one drawing of a particular idea so that he or she can get their point across better.

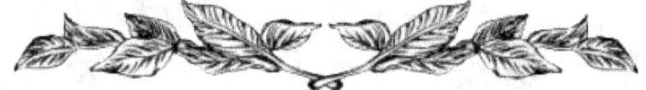

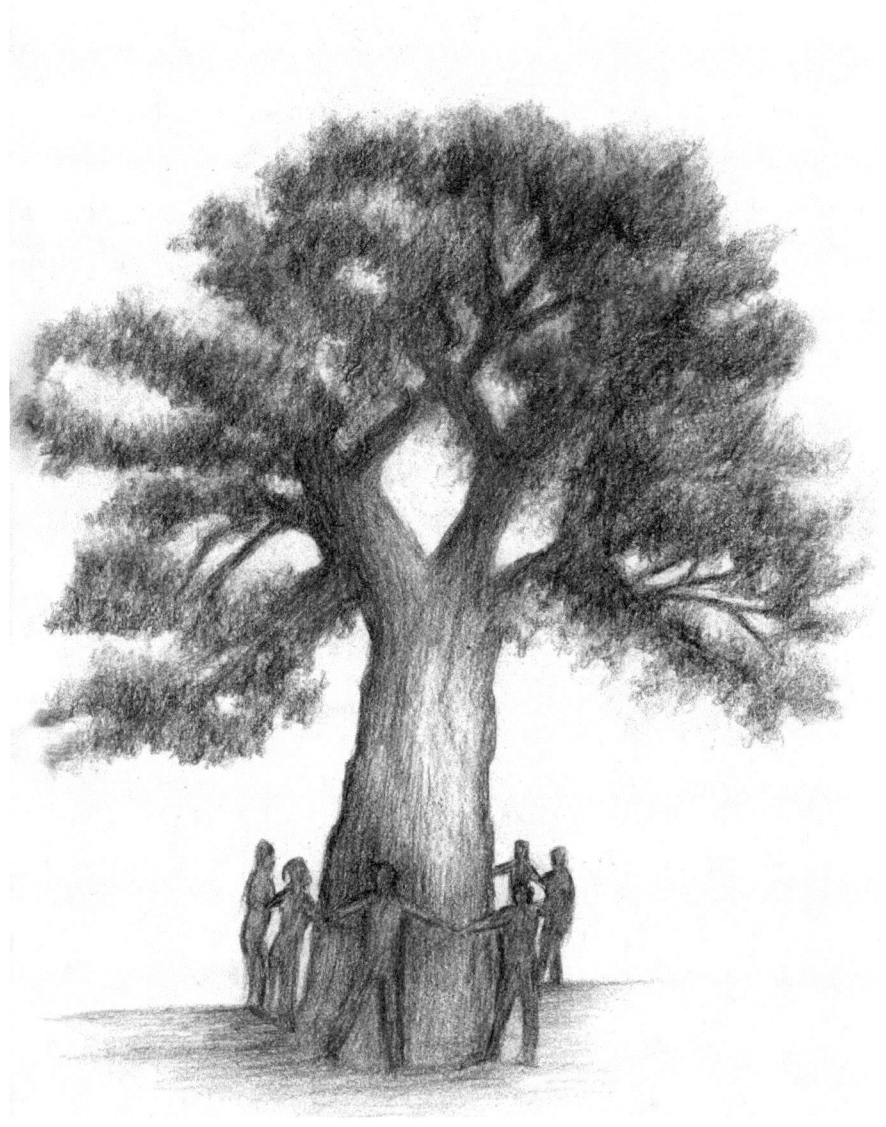

This time people are circling around a tree to signify that there is life to be found with each other as we hold hands. There is a sense of merriment and cheer as the figures are encircling this tree. They are rejoicing in the fact that they are alive and the tree of life pulsates through their veins.

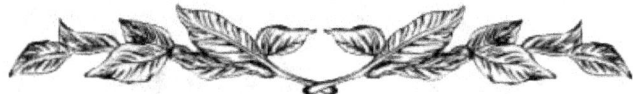

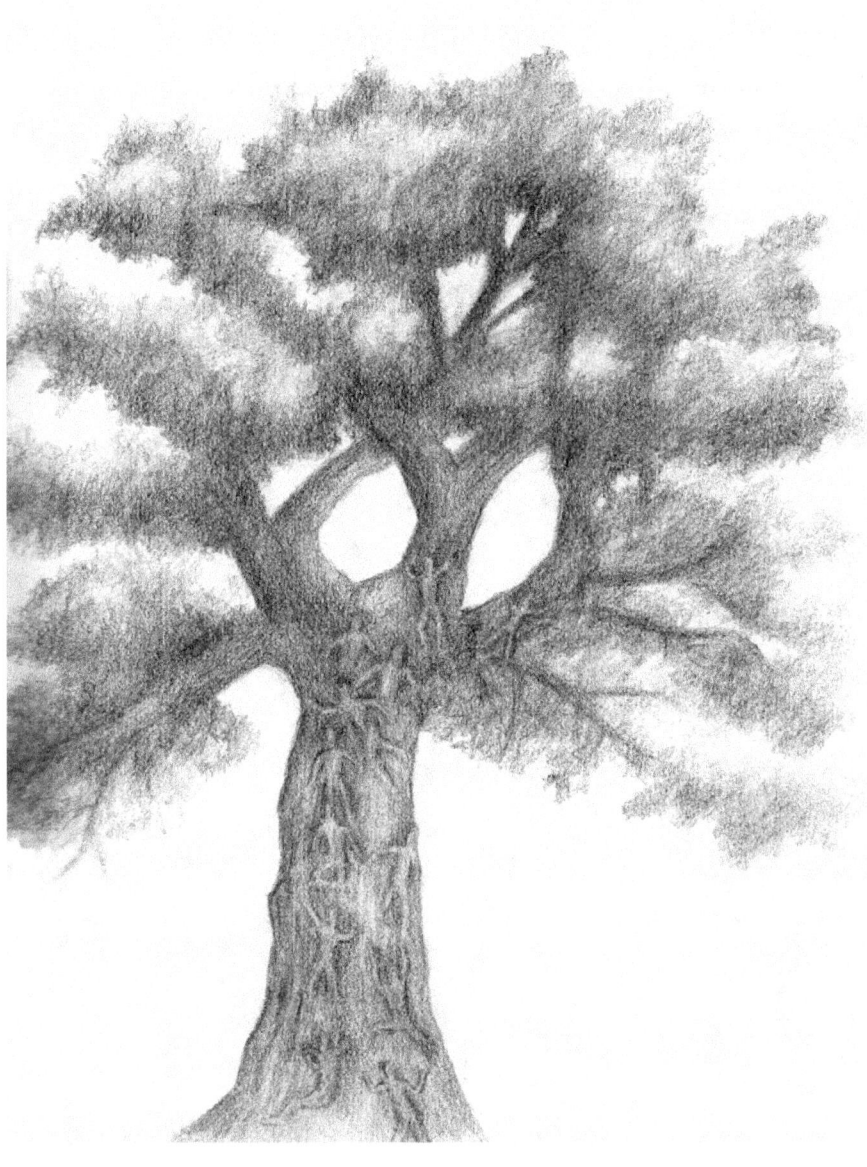

And yet again, I have done another drawing of the tree of life theme. Here once more, figures are seen within the tree rising upwards through the trunk and branches. This one is perhaps more realistic in tone and identifies more truly, how the branches of a large cottonwood tree can contain many things in it even human figures.

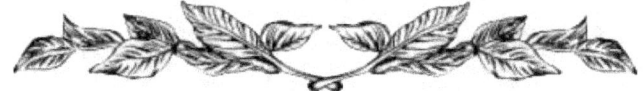

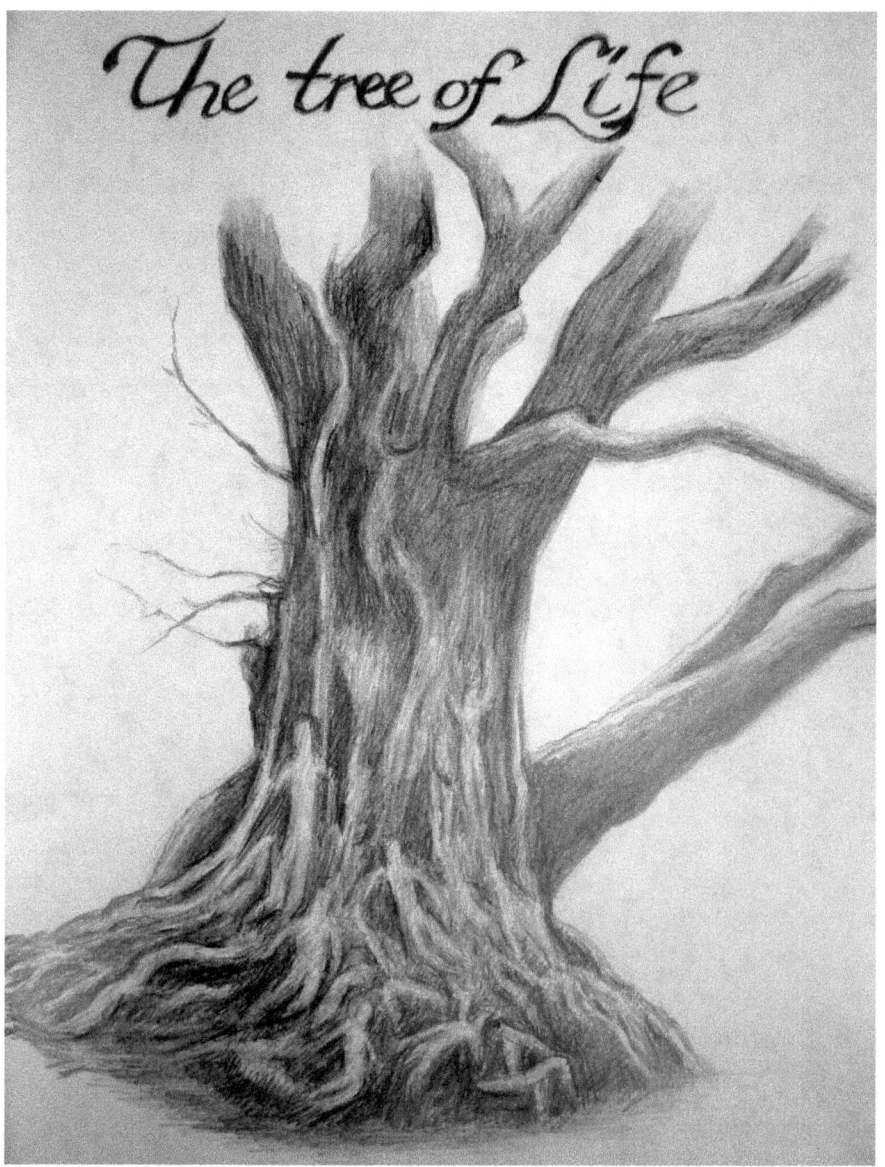

The tree of Life

As one can see, I have found inspiration in this idea of the tree of life. The figures are seen more readily this time around the base of the trunk of the tree rather than further upwards. While there are many different styles that an artist can use at his disposal, as long as he or she can clearly express what they are wanting to say, then they are successful.

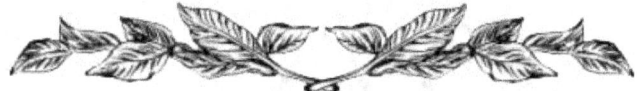

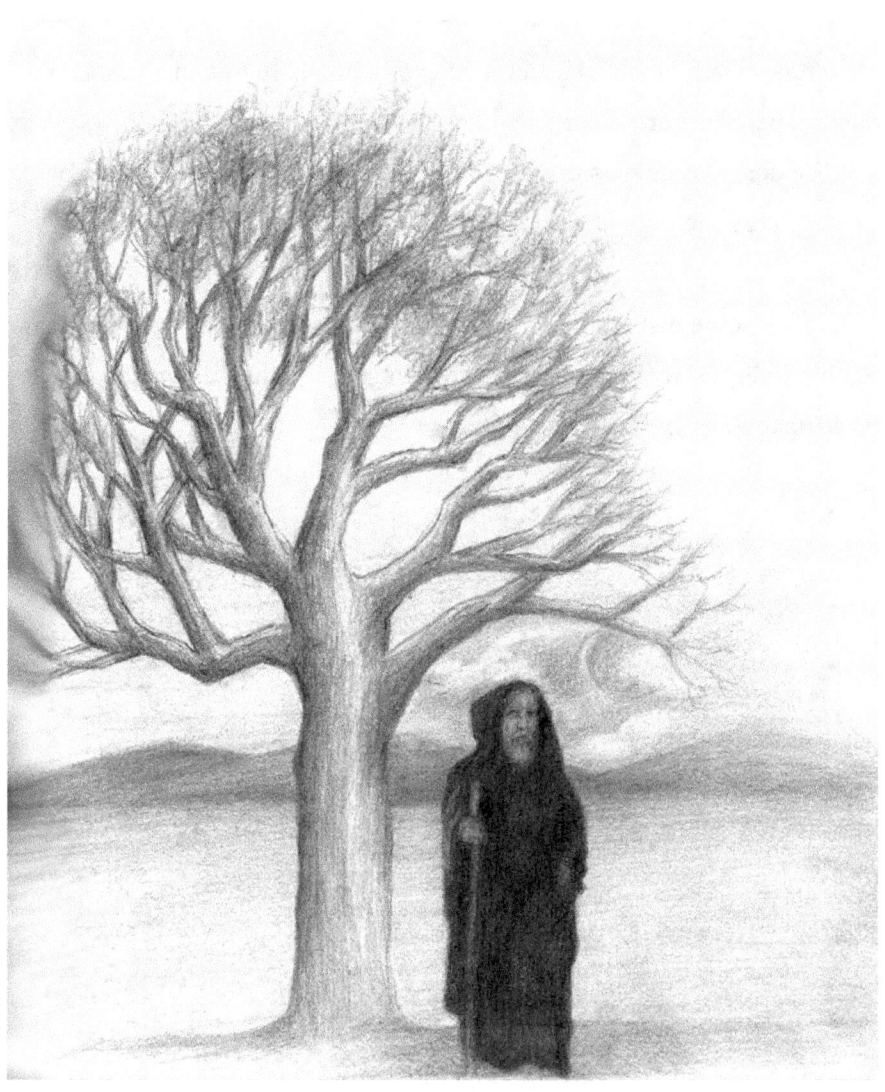

And now finally, there is a simple drawing of a bare tree in a desolate landscape. A figure is seen standing beside this one looking outwards to us. We don't know who he is; perhaps he is just a simple sojourner or maybe a prophet of some kind.

There are some distant hills to be seen in the background and a crescent moon. Everything works together to form a mood that allows the viewer to partake in this.

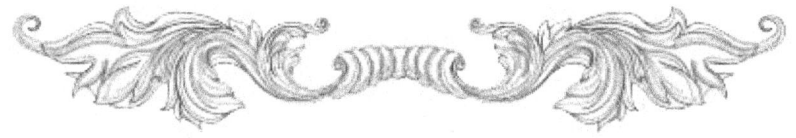

TREES WITH OTHER THINGS

As I have continued to do various drawings of trees in different categories and themes, I decided to add yet another element into the works. In this section, I have endeavored to find different types of objects that can be used in conjunction with the drawing of a tree. Various objects can represent different things to people. Certainly an hourglass would represent the element of time to anyone, and yet I'm certain that hanging hourglasses from a tree is something that is seldom thought of. Of course there is the example of Salvador Dali's famous painting, "The Persistence of Memory."

You will find a piano being played among the trees, a cello that morphs into something else, and a myriad of other ideas. These ideas while being strange to some, hopefully illustrates yet another example of how s simple drawing of a tree can be included with other things. One searches for ideas to use, and in time those concepts come if the artist is patient and decides to go against the norm.

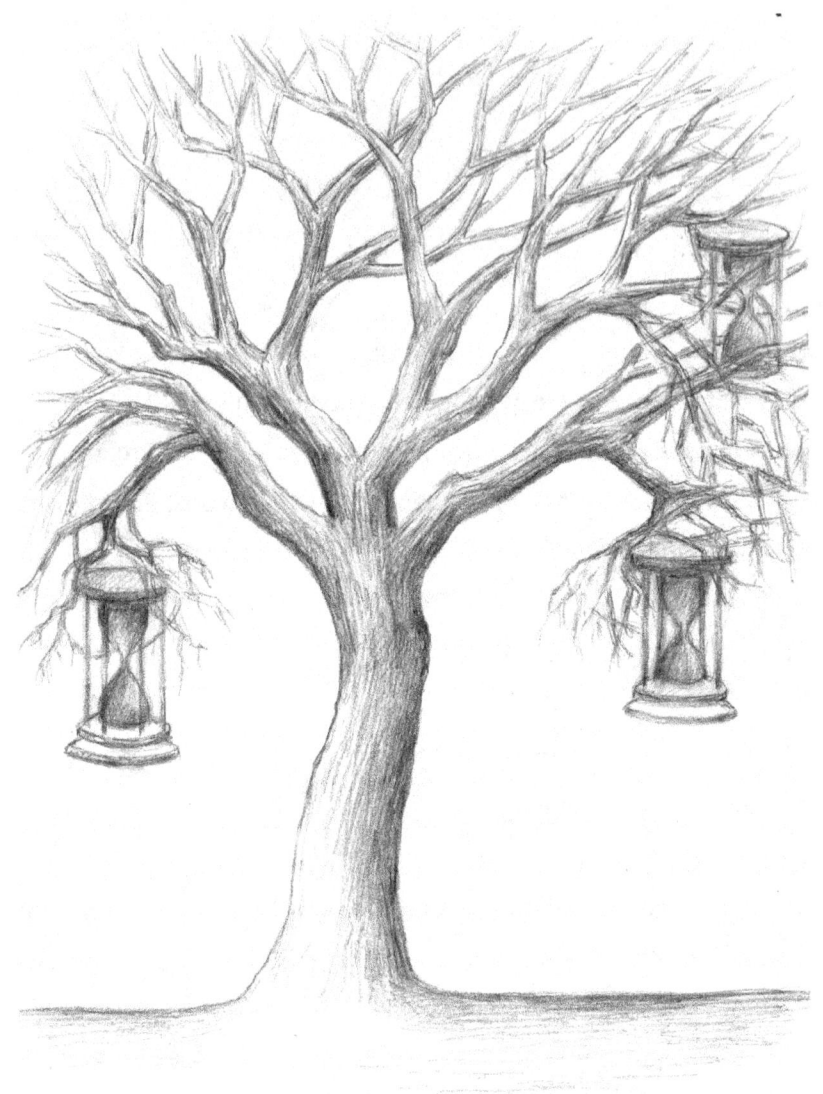

Here is the example of the tree with hourglasses hanging from its branches. There are hundreds and perhaps thousands of different types of time pieces, with each one of them being able to tell time. I have always been struck with the image of an hourglass especially as the sand particles are slowly slipping through its glass enclosure. And yet one can also see how time has had its influence upon nature as the branches and leaves wither and decay. Each and every season demonstrates how time slowly erodes away those things in nature.

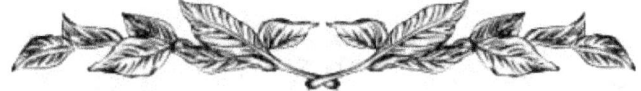

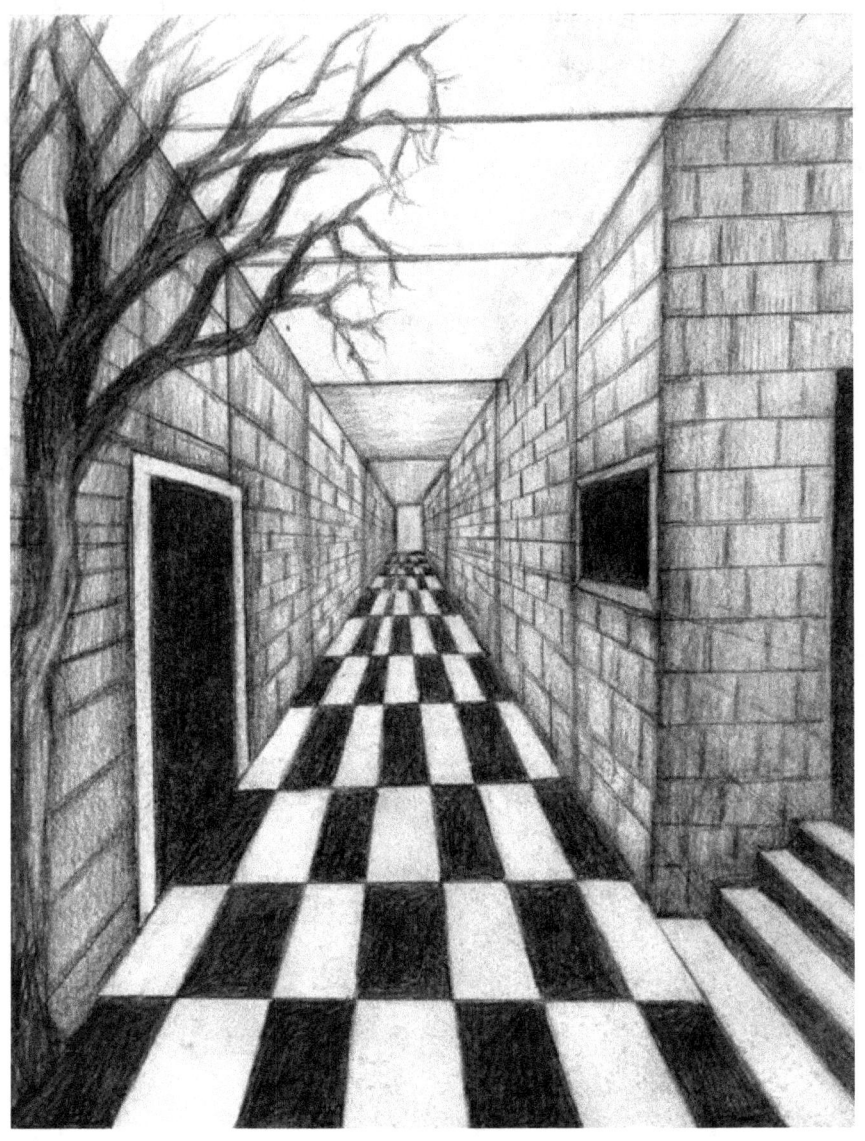

One may find even a tree in the midst of architecture and buildings. In this case, a simple hallway that recedes into the background with its patterns and designs includes a single tree along one of its sections next to the wall. Sometimes buildings have been made alongside nature allowing even a tree to grow-up within the walls of a structure. What better way could there be in order to incorporate what is already there into the framework of what man is attempting to do.

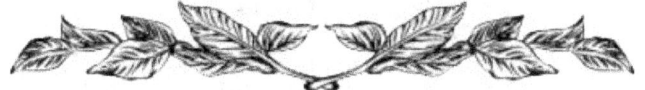

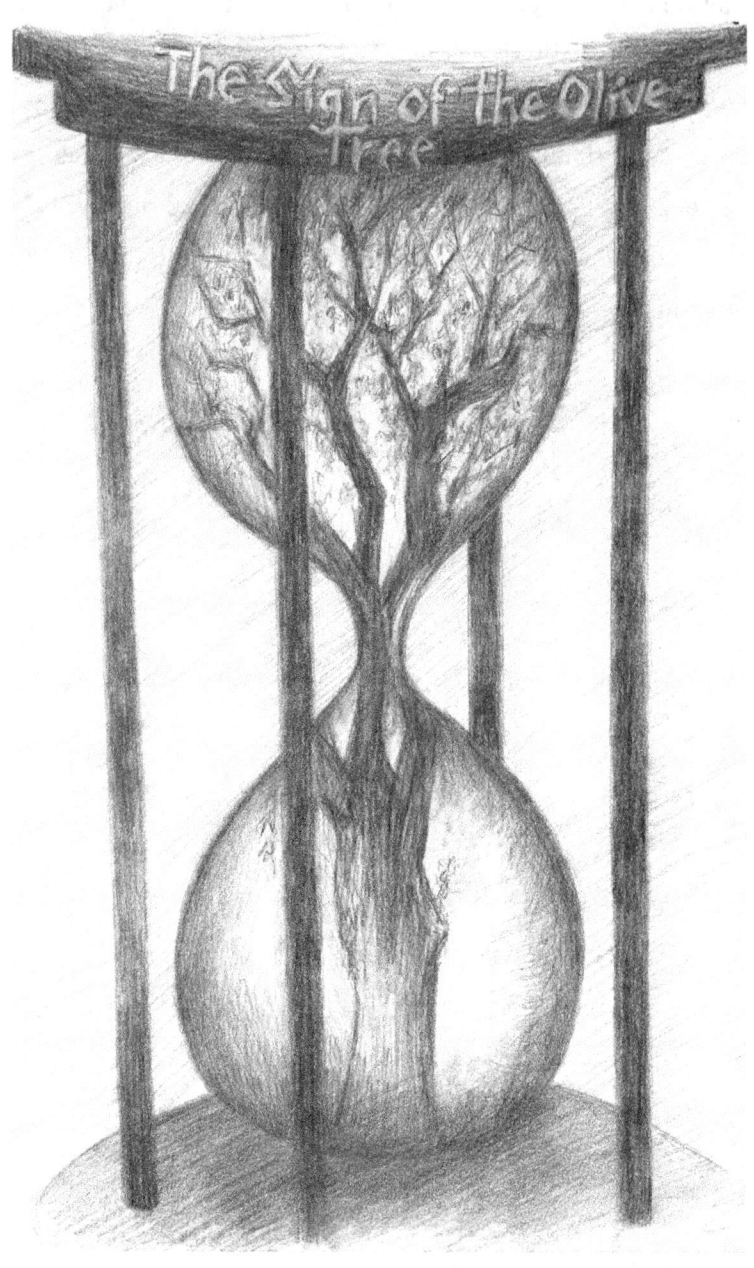

Just as I had used the simple idea of having hourglasses suspended from a tree, now an hourglass has within it a tree spreading forth its branches through the globe. The Olive Tree is a symbol of Israel and so I decided to use that type of tree within the hourglass. Now there is no sand to be seen as it slowly falls through the enclosure, but time itself is now being measured as the Olive Tree itself will come to an end at the culmination of all things.

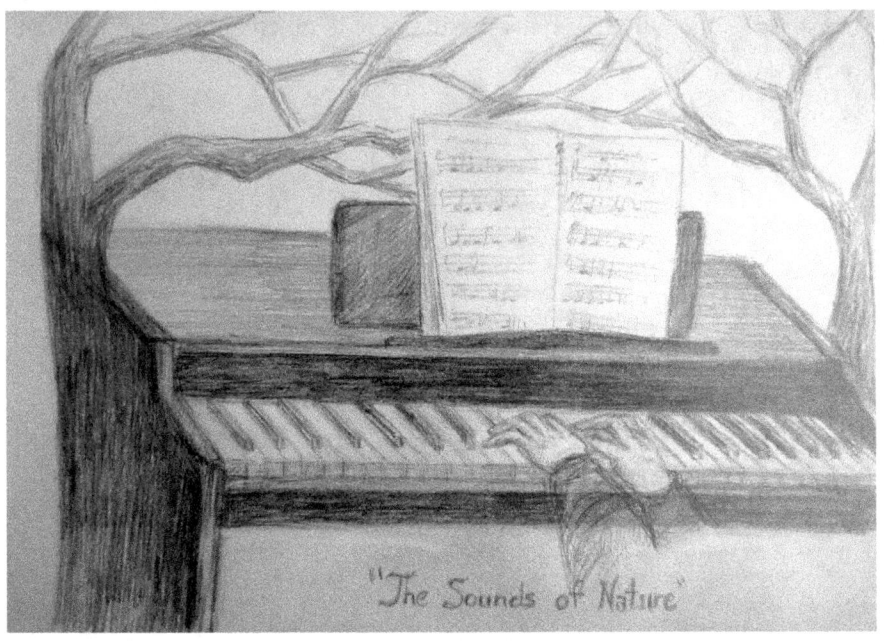

Certainly composers and musicians have been inspired by nature, as we see it in what has been played through the use of musical instruments and songs. My thought here was to have a piano being played outside along the very beauty that perhaps inspired the song that was being played on the piano.

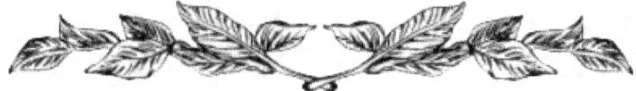

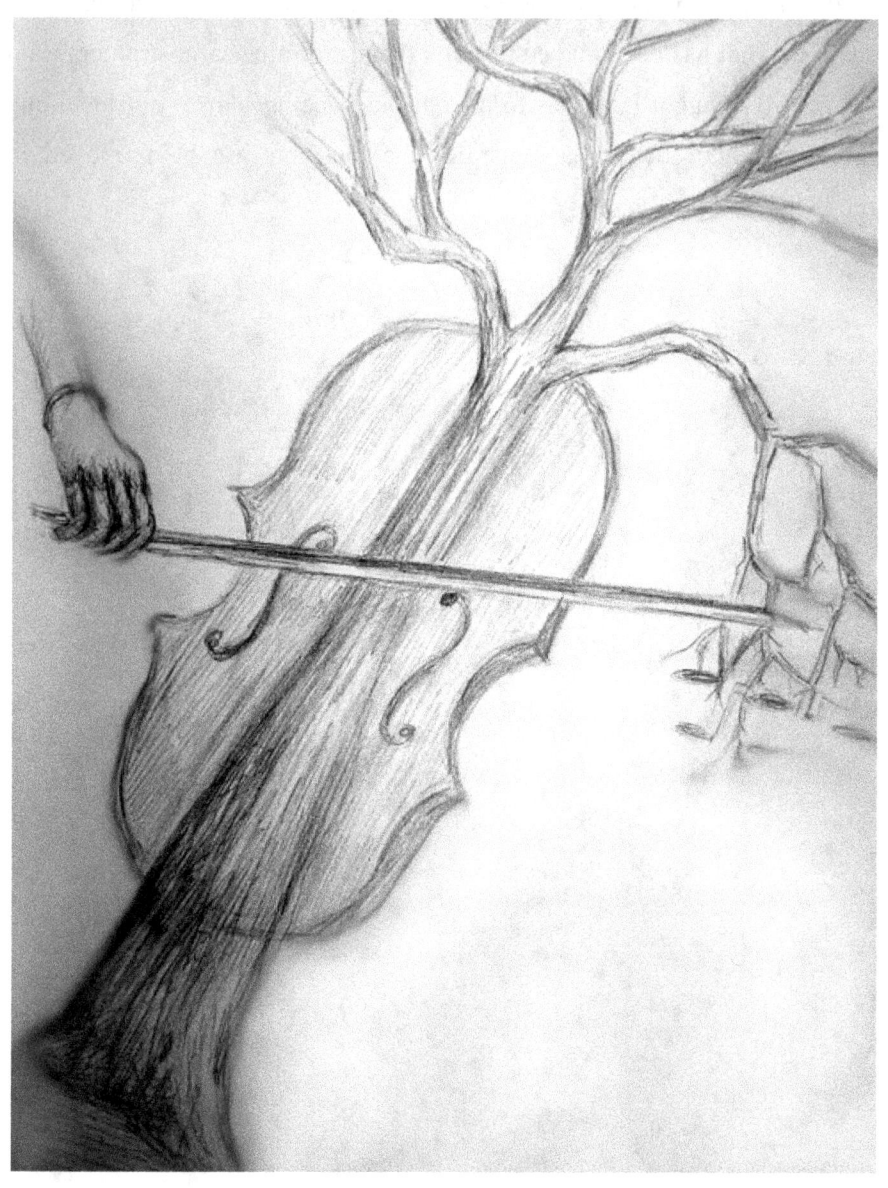

When I was teaching at a high school a few years ago, I did a sketch of someone who was playing a cello. And of course I wanted to incorporate a tree somehow with it. The obvious place seemed to be where the neck of the instrument extended outwards. So, I had the neck of the cello morph into the branch of a tree. Here again, music was being synthesized into nature forming a single unit.

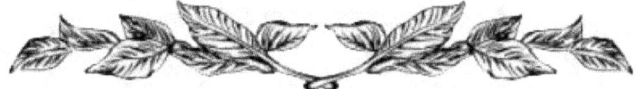

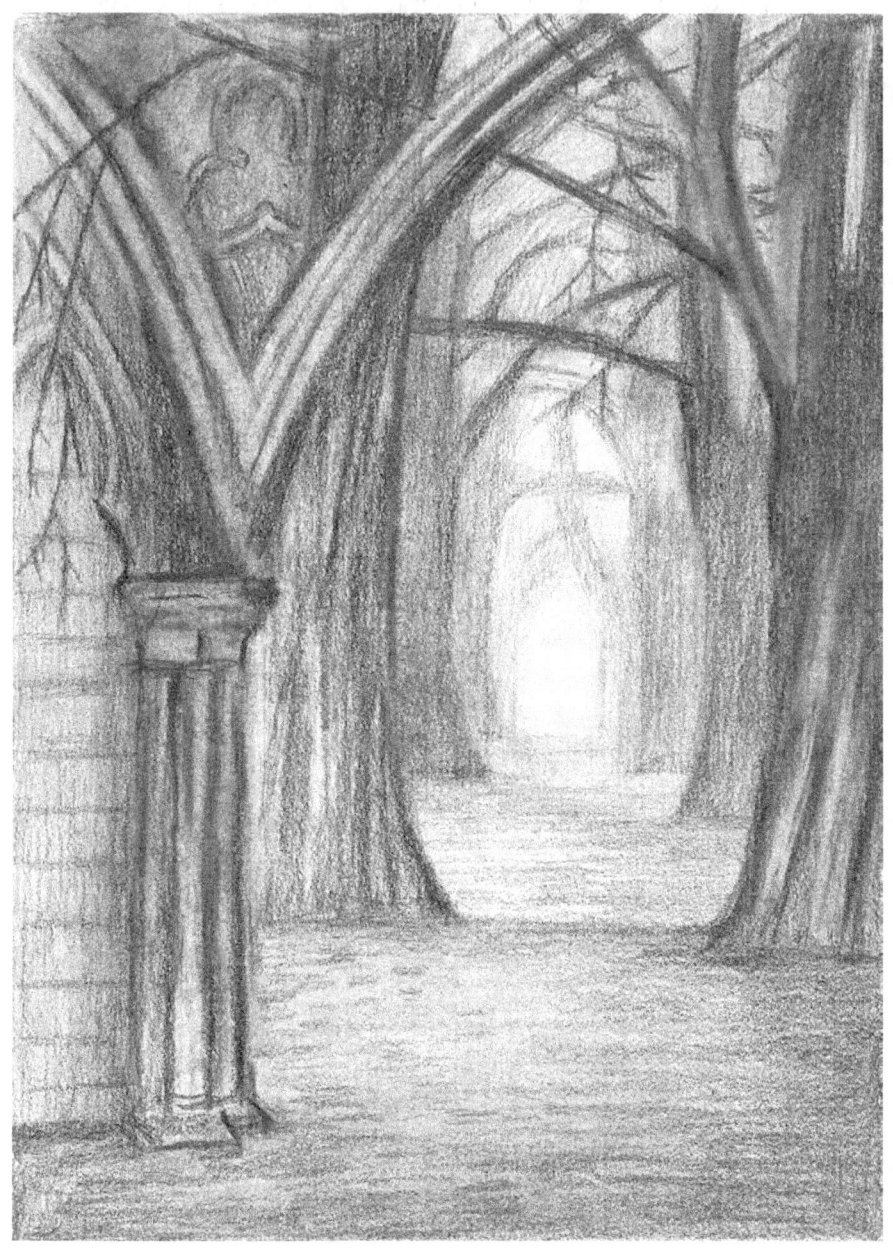

And now architecture is morphing into the branches of trees. The very pillars are blending into the elements of nature seemingly becoming one as they diminish into the background. I have always had an affinity towards ancient architecture and enjoy drawing pillars and the stonework found in temples and other buildings.

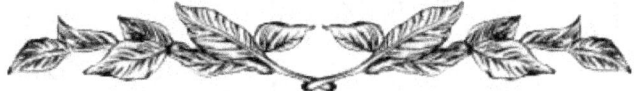

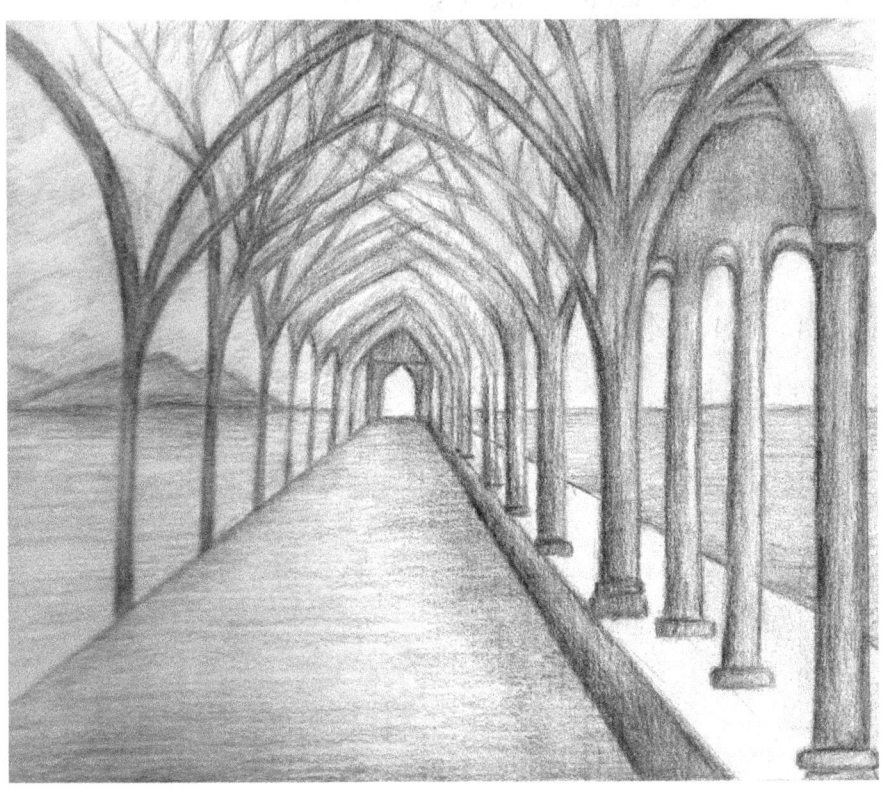

This open-air building with its pillars now blends right into the branches of trees as it recedes into the background of the landscape. The pillars and tree trunks are somewhat similar in their shapes in that they have a trunk that is the main structural element in them. Of course pillars are straight and don't have any variance or bent limbs as part of their overall structure. But pillars themselves are tapered and can be designed anyway that they may be intended.

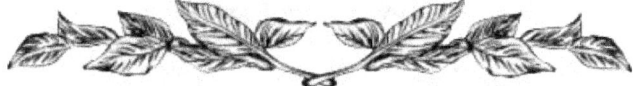

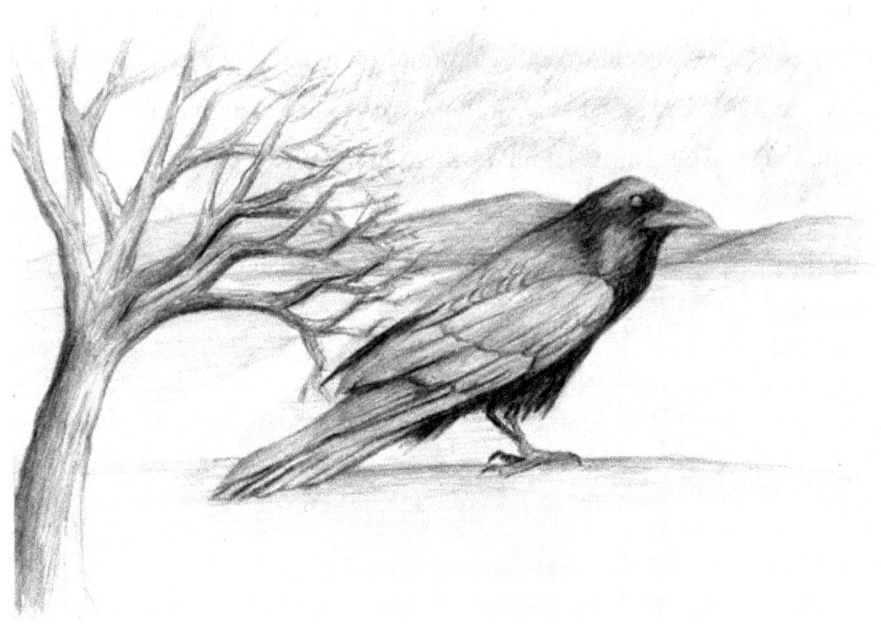

And here now is a simple raven beside an old weathered tree. Over the years I've done many drawings similar this one because for some reason, the two seem to go hand-in-hand with each other forming as it were, a single unit. Sometimes simplicity is key to creating a scene that is pleasing to the eye and still complete in its execution.

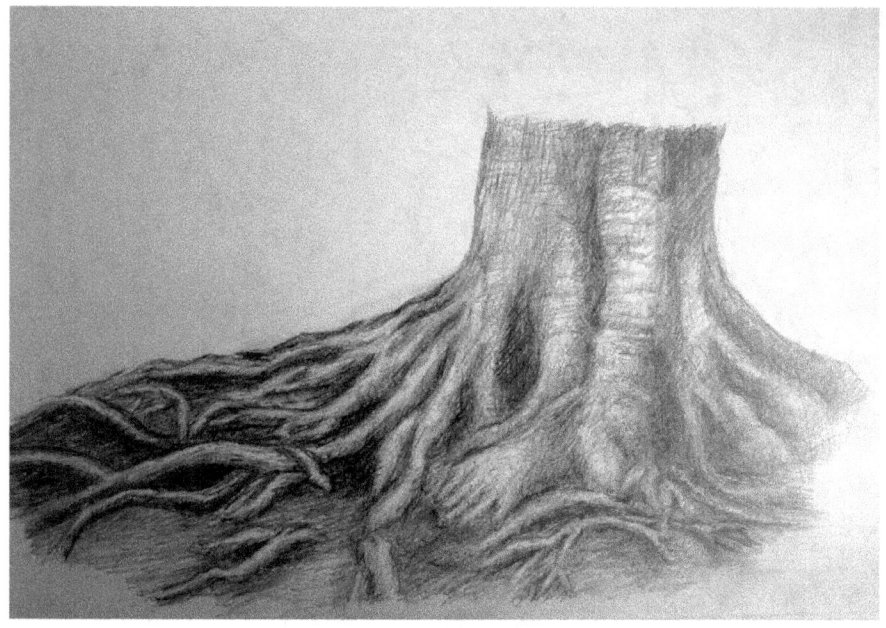

Sometimes if one would look at the roots of a tree they might see patterns or also perhaps other things. In this case, perhaps you see a hand as it rests among the roots. To be sure it would be a very strange thing to see, and yet it isn't meant to be scary or morbid, but just the intertwining of two elements into one.

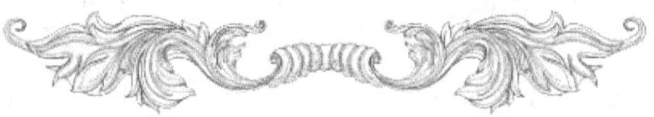

JUST TREES

Of course what would a book of drawings of trees be without simply doing a drawing of one of them unadorned without changing anything? There are so many different types of trees in the world, and one could spend a lifetime drawing them.

Actually, the more twisted and unique the tree is, the more I am fascinated by it. In my walks and time alone, I have seen some very unusual and wonderful-looking trees. Each and every one of them is beautiful in its own right. In some ways, trees are like people because they are so different and there is not a single one of them like another one.

I could continue drawing hundreds of trees in this section and yet there are a few other sections to be included in this book of trees. For now though, enjoy the simple drawings of various trees here.

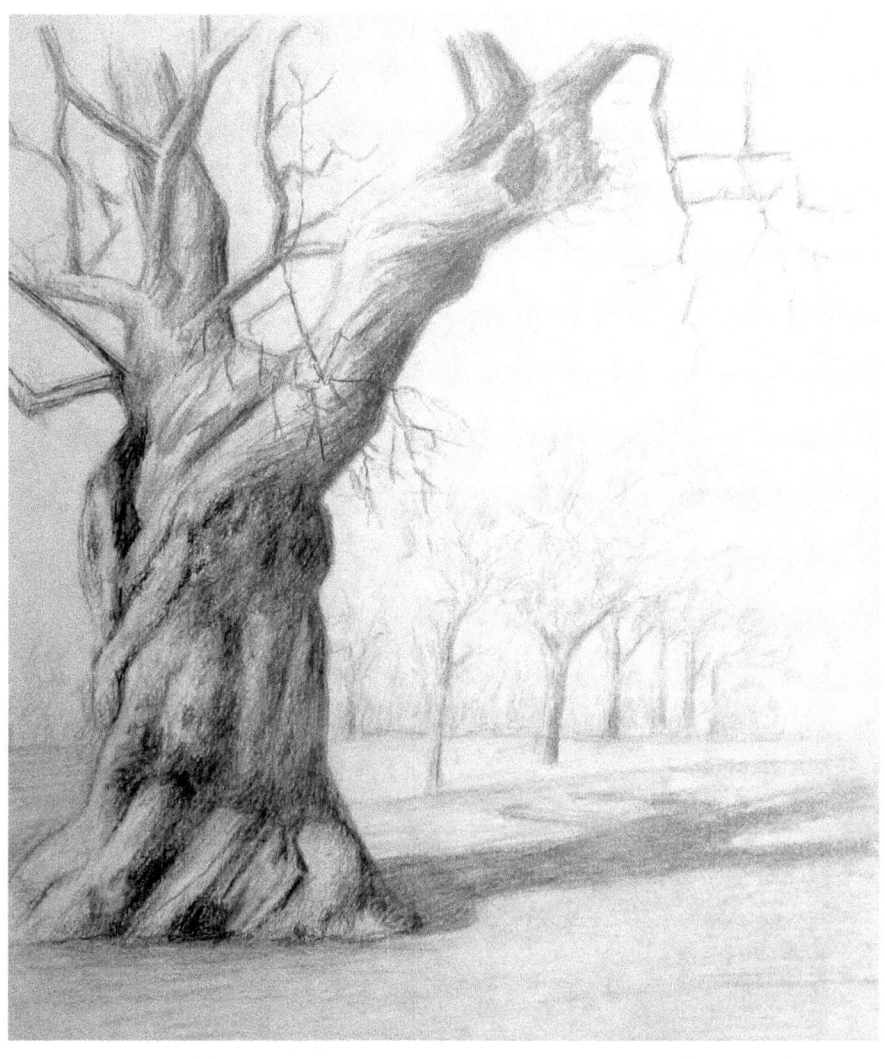

I found this tree while walking years ago nearby a home that we lived in. I can't remember what time of the year it was, but I was struck by the contours and overall shape of the limbs and trunk. The tree itself seemed to signify strength and wisdom to me. It exhibited volume as each limb climbed upwards to the sky.

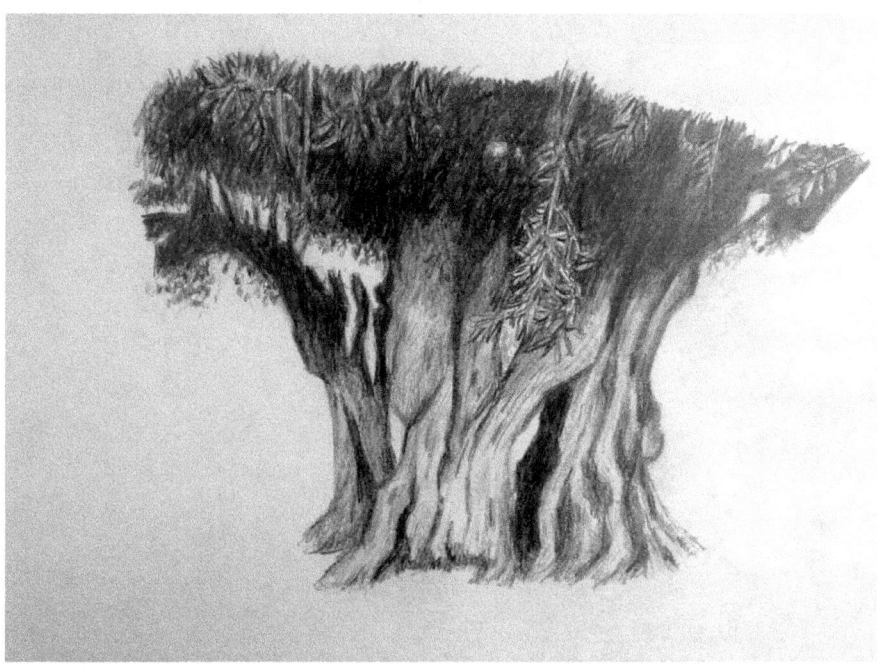

There was a great sense of rustic texture that I saw in this portion of a tree. The trunk itself was in contrast to the leafy, tender quality of foliage. I can't remember if this was part of the root of a tree or just the bottom portion of the tree itself.

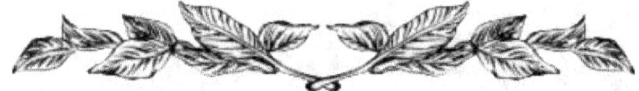

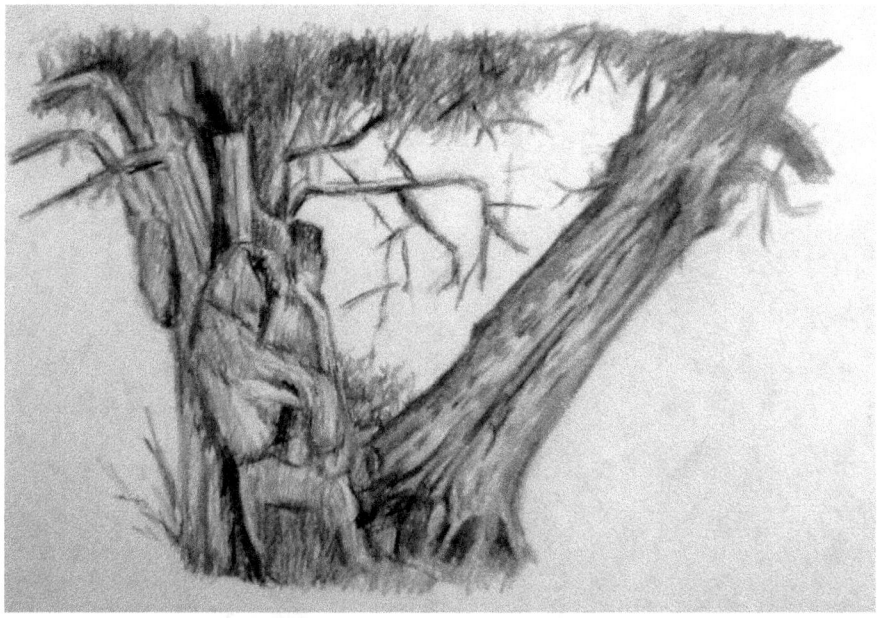

Two limbs rose out from the base of this tree. It almost had a stony appearance that exhibited endurance. It was a windy day and yet the tree stood erect as if nothing would ever move it from its place. Wouldn't it be great if we had this type of endurance and strength like that of a tree?

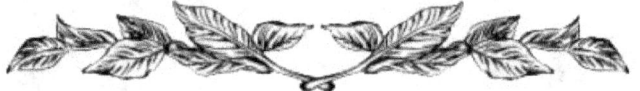

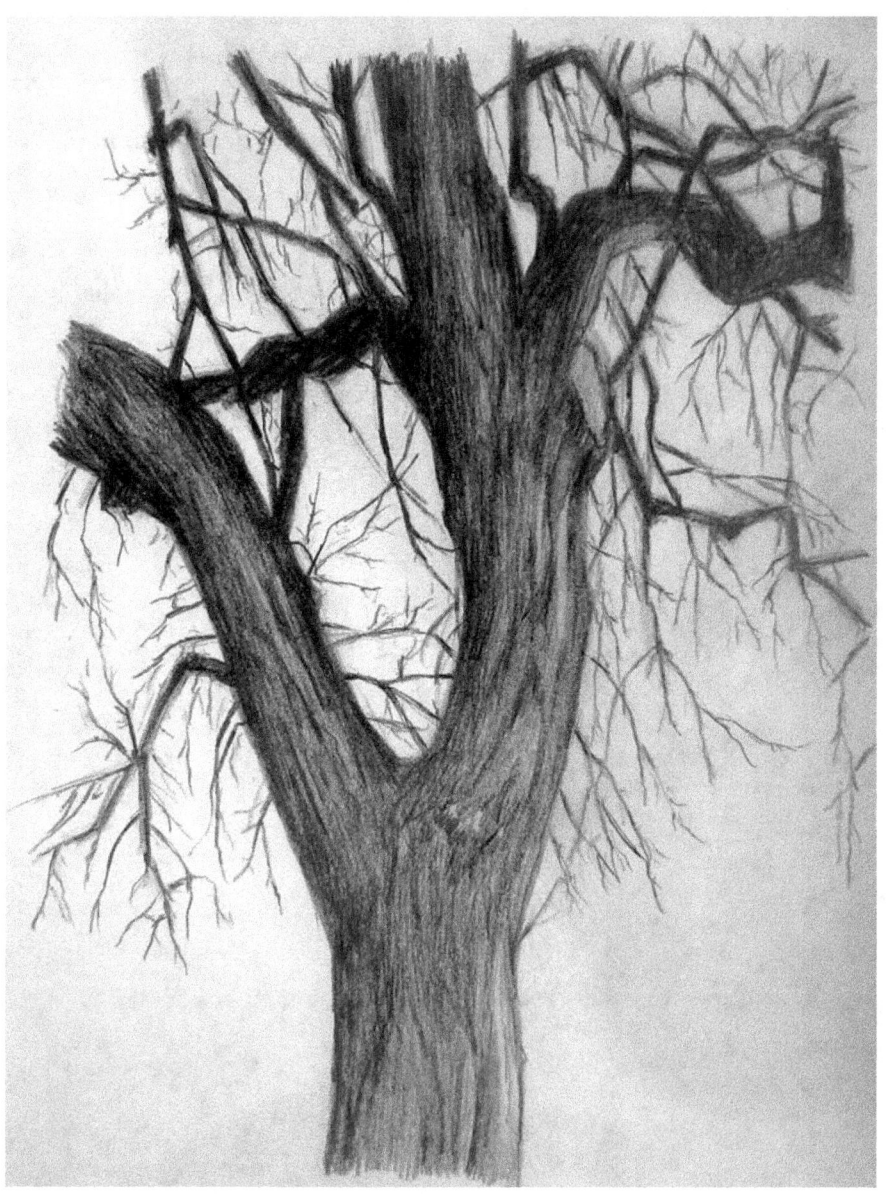

This is a portion of a huge cottonwood tree that was nearby our home years ago. I always noticed it as I passed by on the way to somewhere else. Throughout each season it always exhibited the same timeless quality that I remember. I often wondered how old it was and what it might have said to those who passed by it.

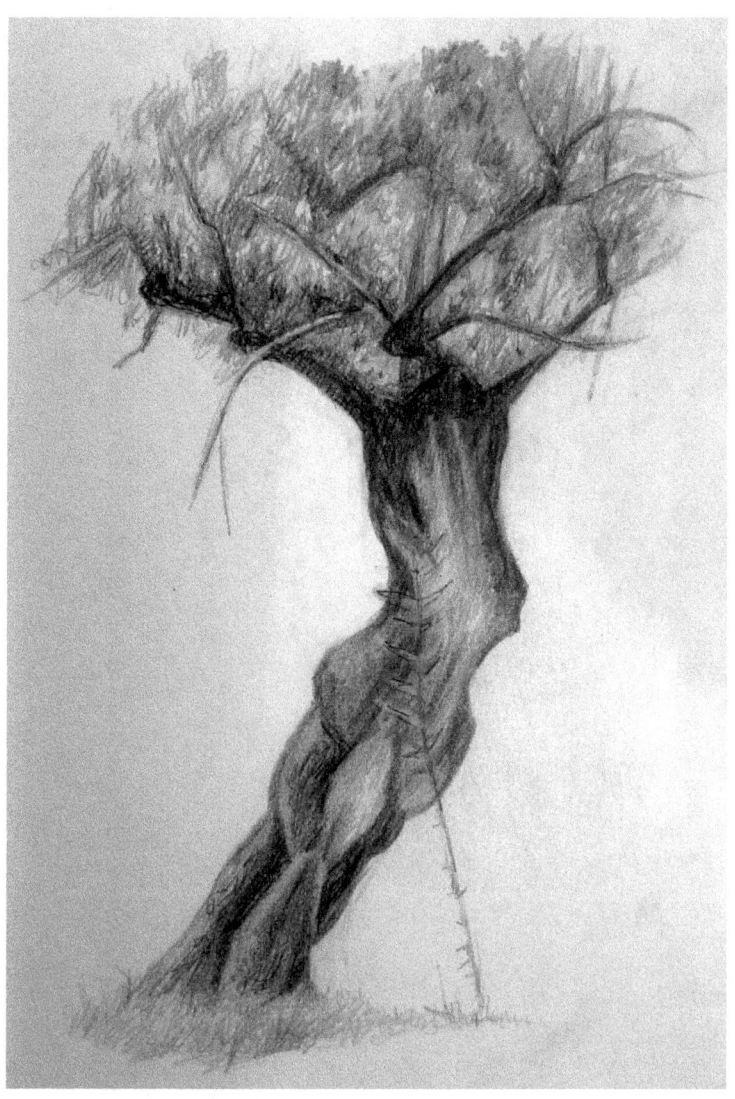

This tree seemed to almost be dancing in the wind as it swayed back and forth. In some ways it was almost like a musical instrument; perhaps a flute playing some kind of melody from its branches. And yet probably there is a music to be heard that comes forth as one is in nature.

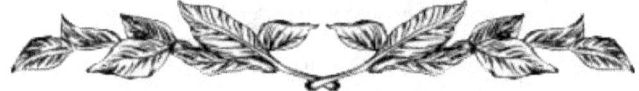

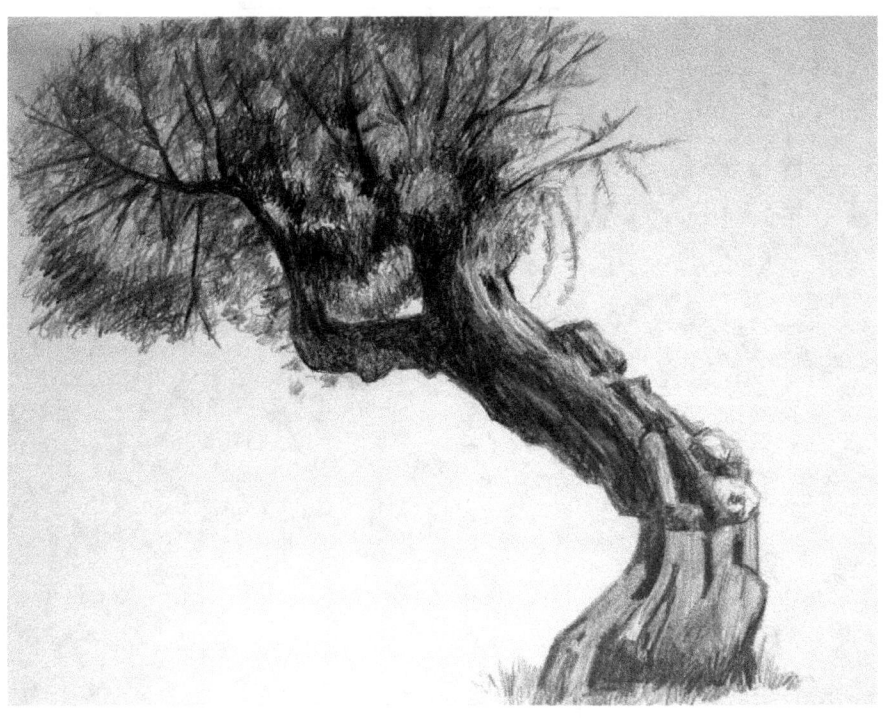

Here yet is another tree that exhibited strength and resolve. The trunk and limbs on this one seemed to show a chiseled look in the deep grooves of the bark. Sometimes a tree is almost like a sculpture in how its form is seen. This one is very much like that.

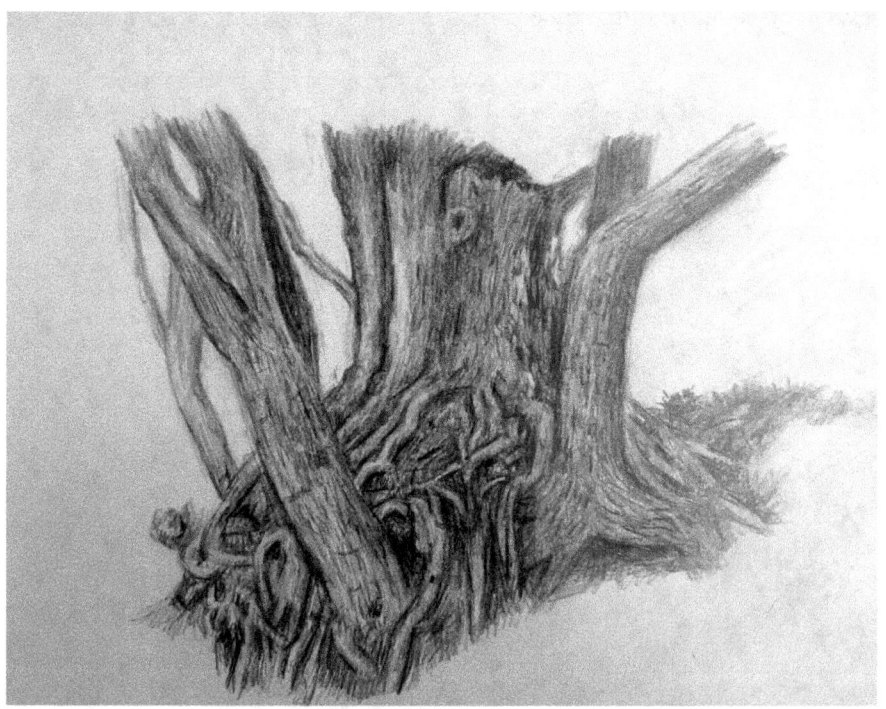

Sometimes there are aspects that are seen in a tree that look like other things. In this case the winding shapes around the base look almost like writhing snakes or tubes of some sort. Nature has a way of showing aspects of beauty and at other times, even the grotesque or strange is seen.

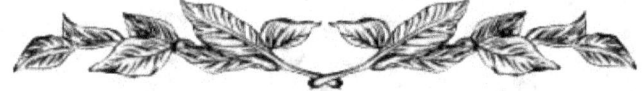

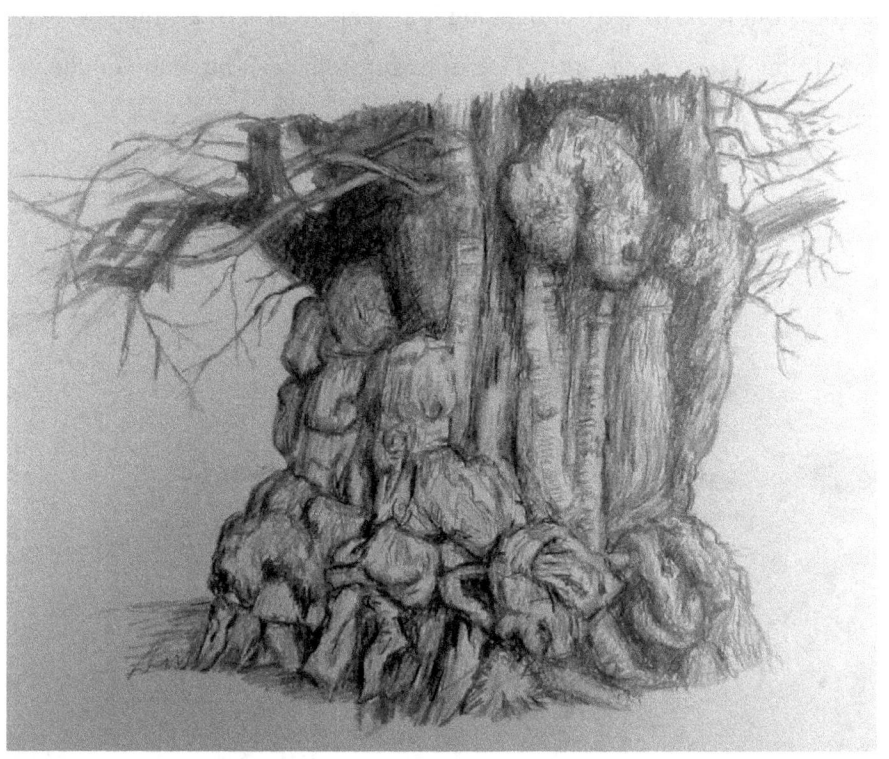

Sometimes the trunk of a tree has shapes in it that don't seem to belong with the rest of it. In this case, circular projections were spread throughout most of the trunk giving it the appearance of a strange skin condition. There are a wide range of textures that can be found on the surface of a tree just like there are with the skin of a person.

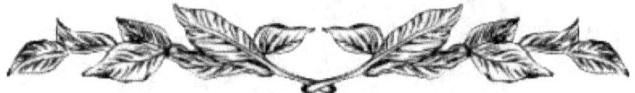

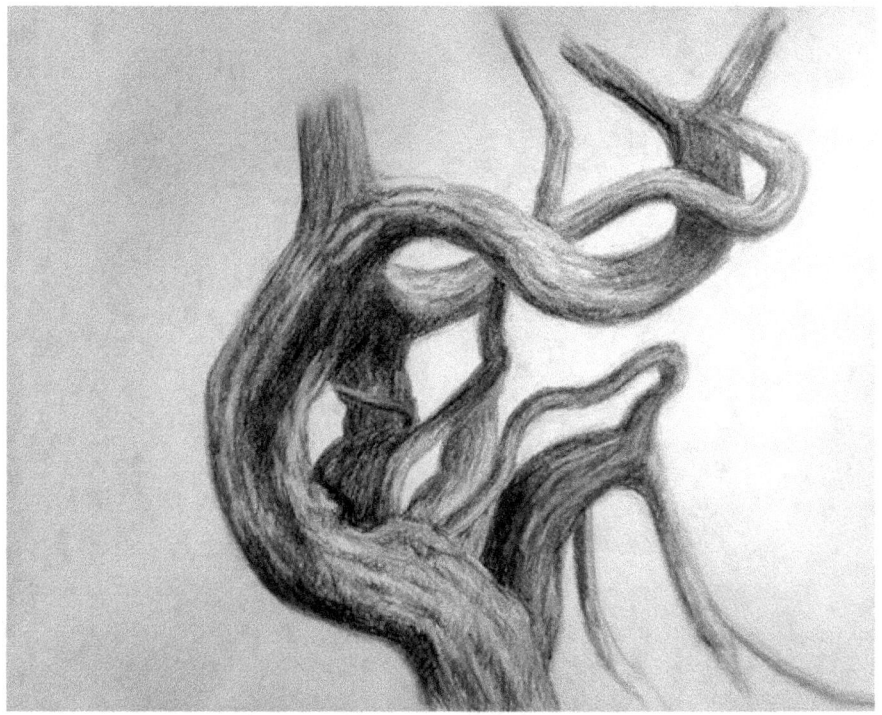

Sometimes the shape of a tree takes on the writhing form of a curving snake or reptile. There was so much character in these limbs that I had to capture what I had seen. One of the most important things I consider when doing a drawing of a tree is the type of character that it exhibits to me. If a tree looks like all the other ones around it then there is no reason for me to draw it.

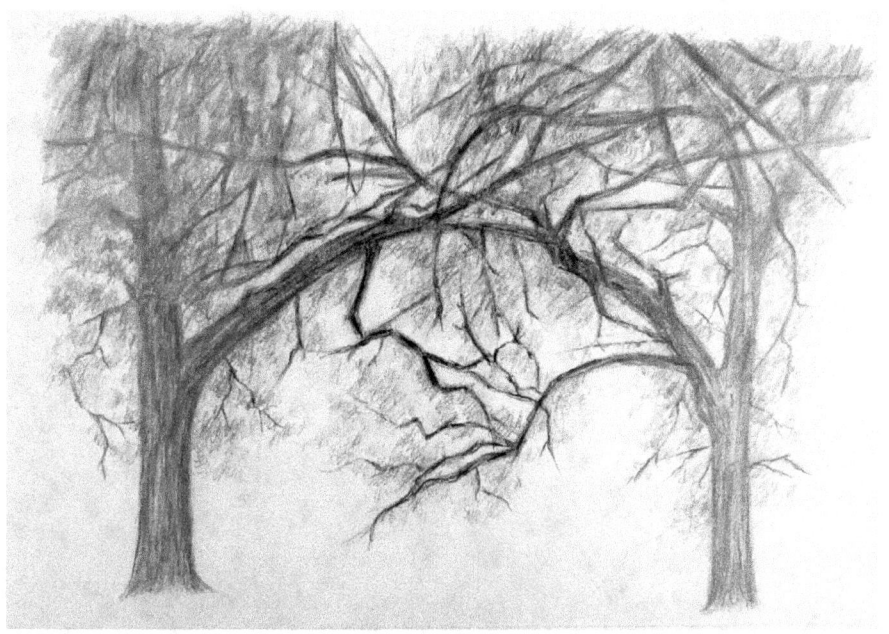

This previous tree had a tree on either side that formed an arch that connected both of them. Just as with people, perhaps even nature finds a way of joining with others of a like mind so that it will become one in essence. Even with all of the differences that are inherent in nature, there is a beauty to be found there that comprises and holds each and every part together.

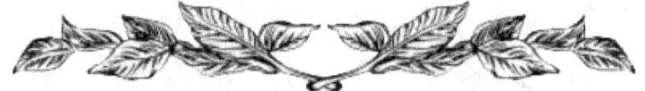

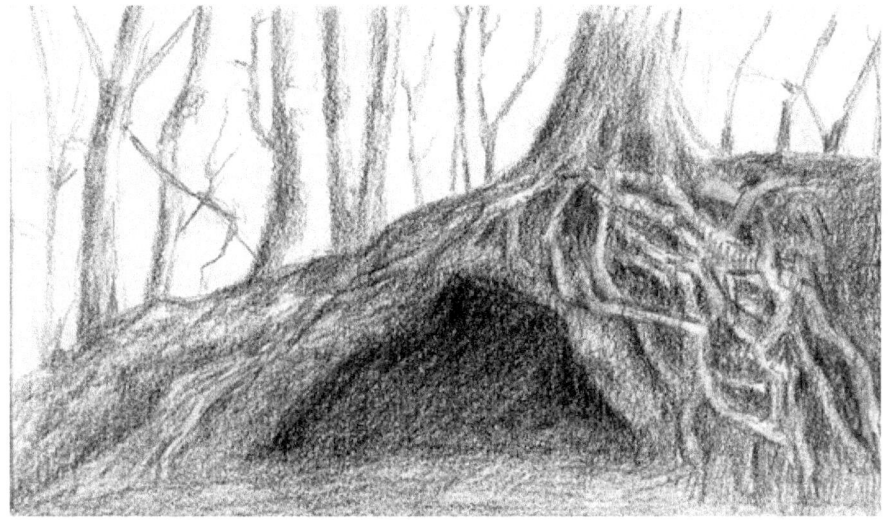

I used this drawing in a book that I had done a few years ago. This particular drawing was to identify a cave where some treasure had been hidden. Oftentimes people have buried things in caves where no one would find them. Caves also represent a place of mystery where the darkness hides what is within.

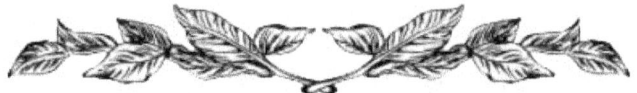

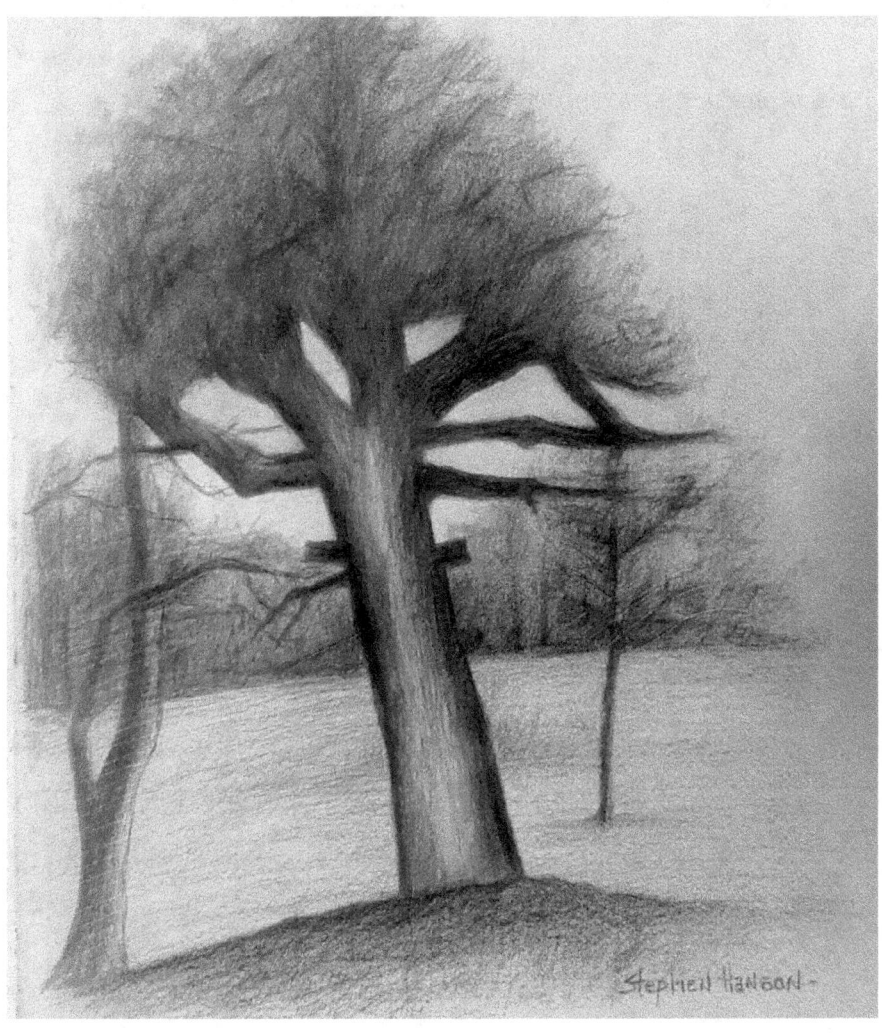

I did this drawing recently when we were camping up in the mountains in Colorado. There were many Ponderosa Pines around but this one had unusual limbs and projections coming out of it. Someone had cut off a few of the limbs giving them a square-like appearance. The original drawing had orange and reddish tones in the trunk as many Ponderosa Pines typically do.

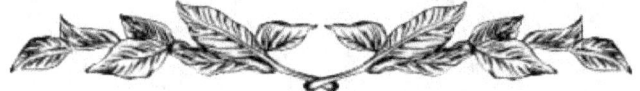

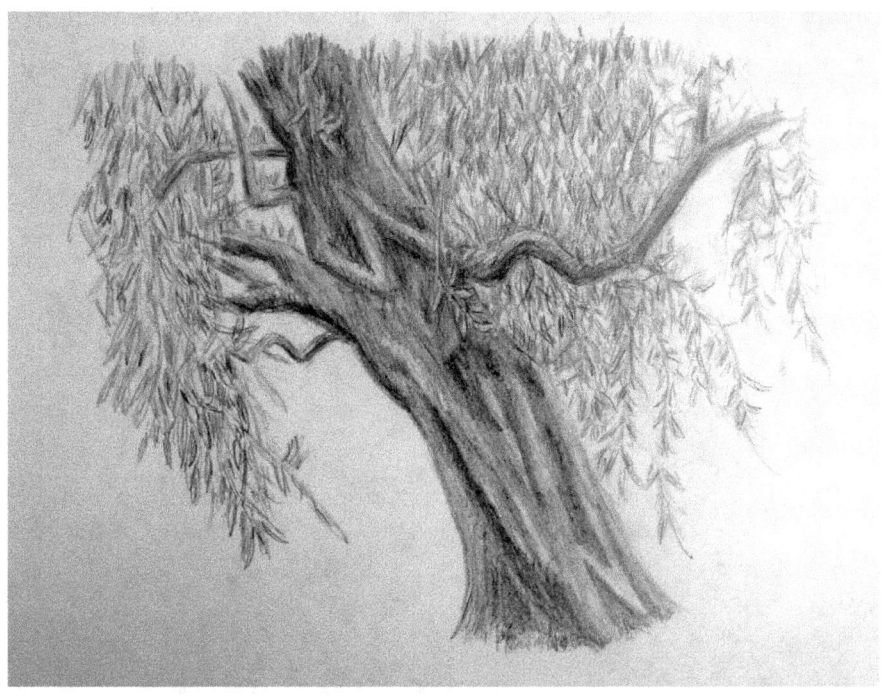

This particular drawing had a musical-like appearance as it was blowing in the wind. The tree itself was bent off to one side almost like a human figure. The willow leaves stood in sharp contrast to the woody grain of the trunk. Sometimes there is a delicacy in some parts of a tree as well as a stony strength.

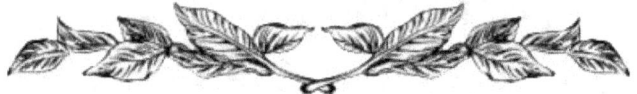

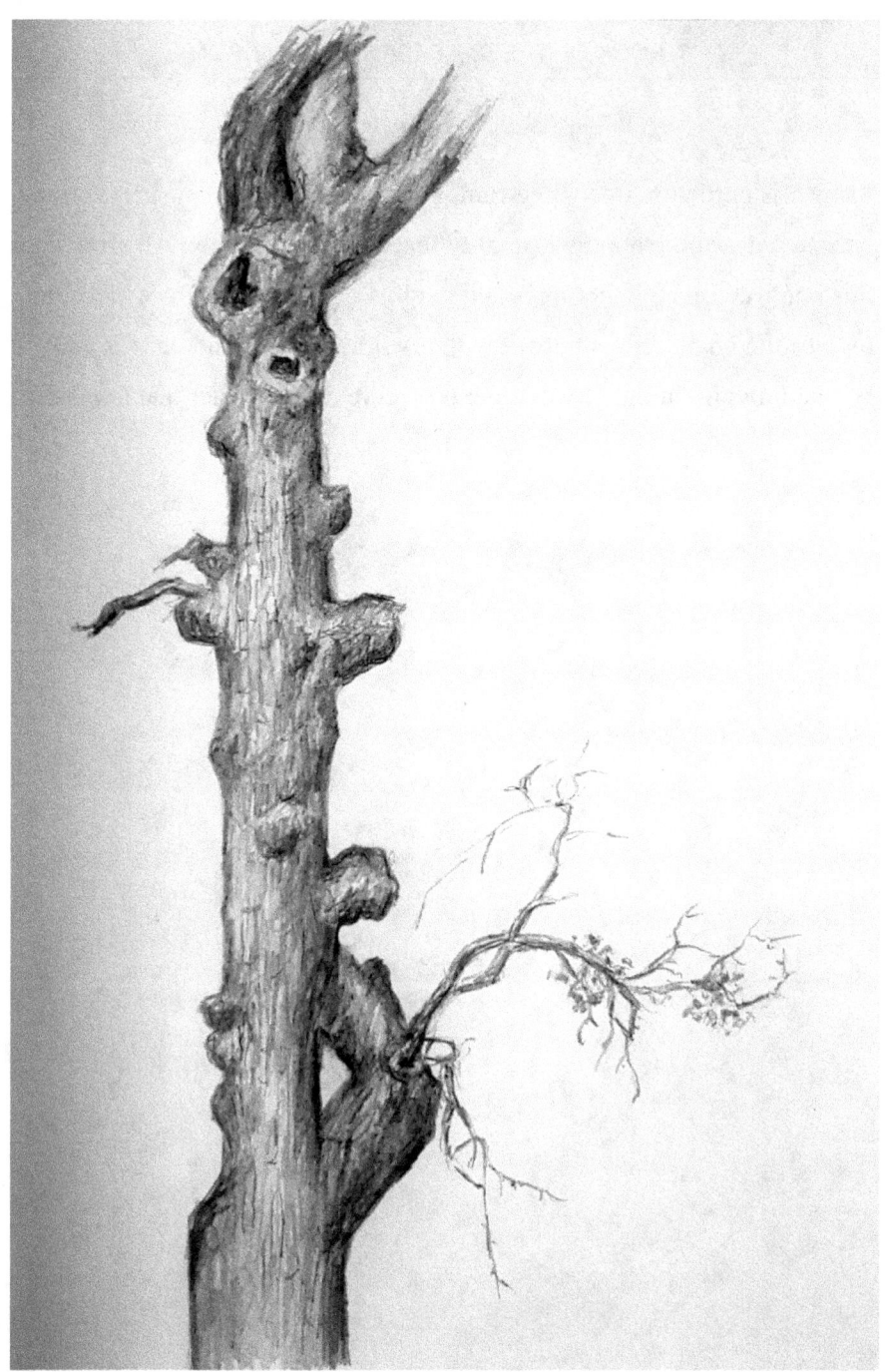

I saw this particular tree while camping recently. It had unusual sections on it and it exhibited a rustic quality that I wanted to draw. All around this one were many other trees and yet this one stood out from all of the rest. I found a place to sit down with my drawing pad and pencils and began drawing. In time I was able to capture the character that I wanted to.

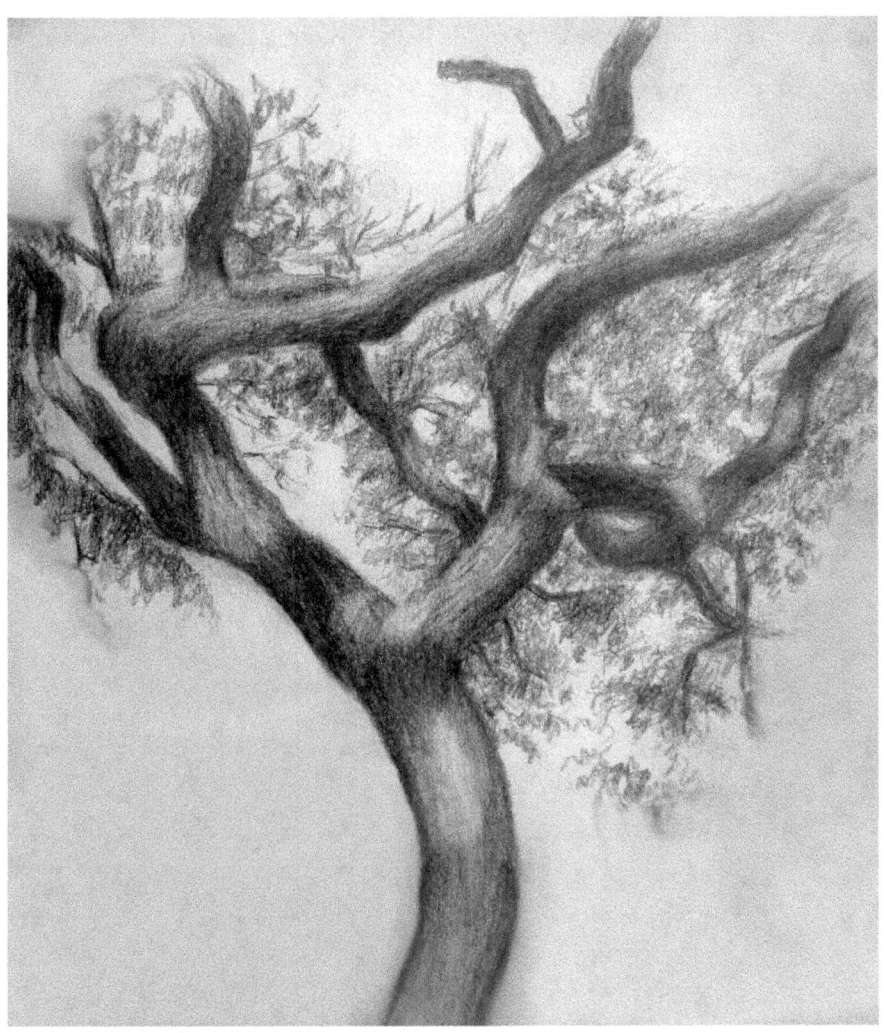

This is another tree that I saw when we were camping in Texas. I was struck by its sweeping curves and lines. The light that fell upon it gave the contours a strong three-dimensional appearance. The artist always needs to see how the elements of his work fit into a pleasing composition and give the viewer a way to enter in as well.

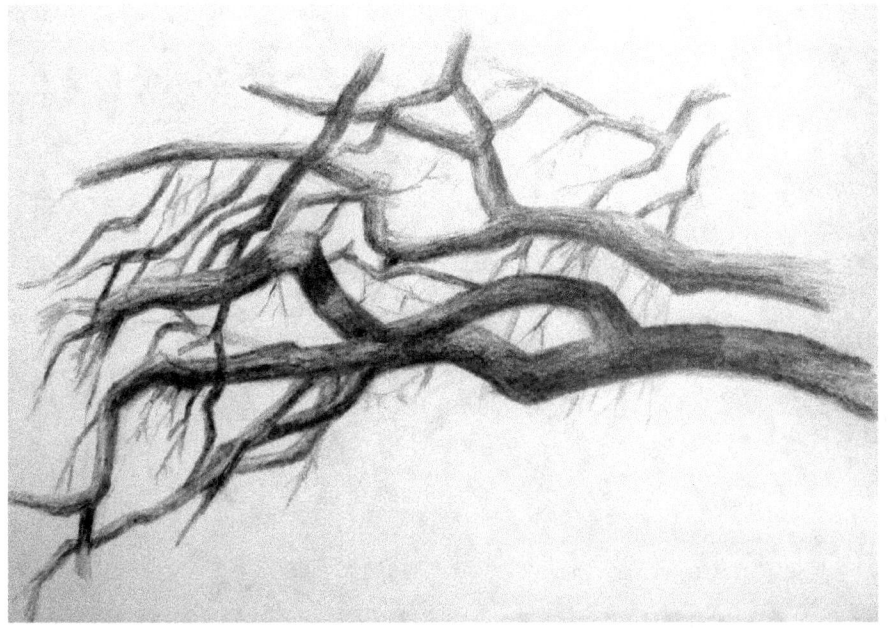

Sometimes it is just the branches of a tree that have inspired me. As I looked at the overall appearance of the tree my sight was focused primarily upon the extremities. There were many branches and twigs on this year but I needed to focus upon the main ones that were seen. The artist learns how to simply those things that are oftentimes very complex.

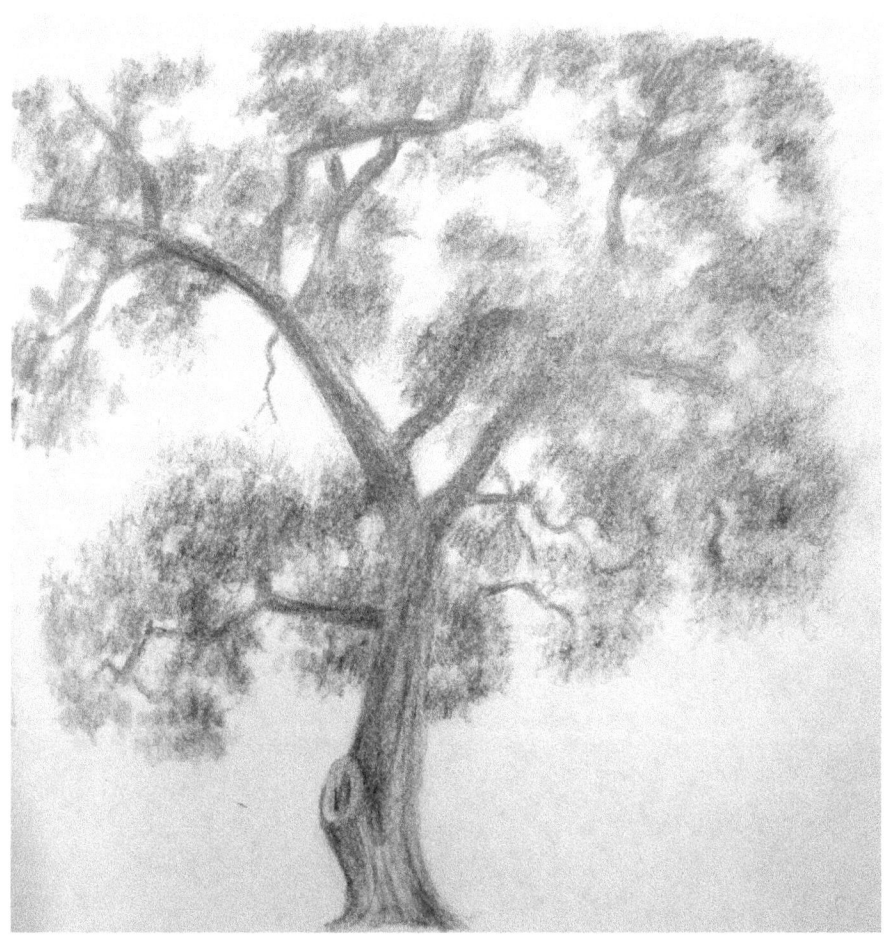

In Texas there are a variety of different types of trees and many of them are oaks. Oak trees have always exhibited strength and resolve to me and also beauty and character.

I believe that oak trees are probably one of my favorite types of trees. I intend to continue to draw as well as paint them in various settings.

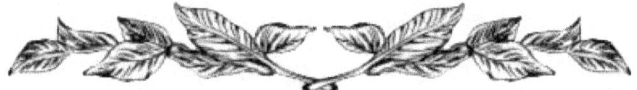

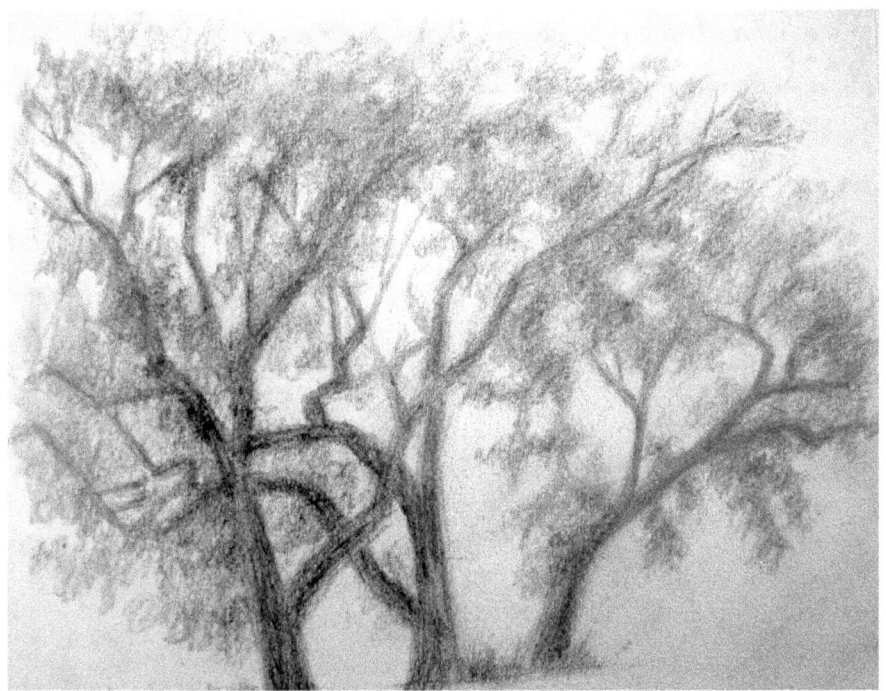

Just as there was a single oak tree there are also groupings of them.
There are a multitude of different arrangements of trees and each of them
exhibit their own individual characteristics. We found a beautiful place
to stay for a while down here in southern Texas next to San Antonio.
Some of these trees have moss hanging from them and others don't.
There are many different varieties of oak trees and each one of them is
unique in their own way.

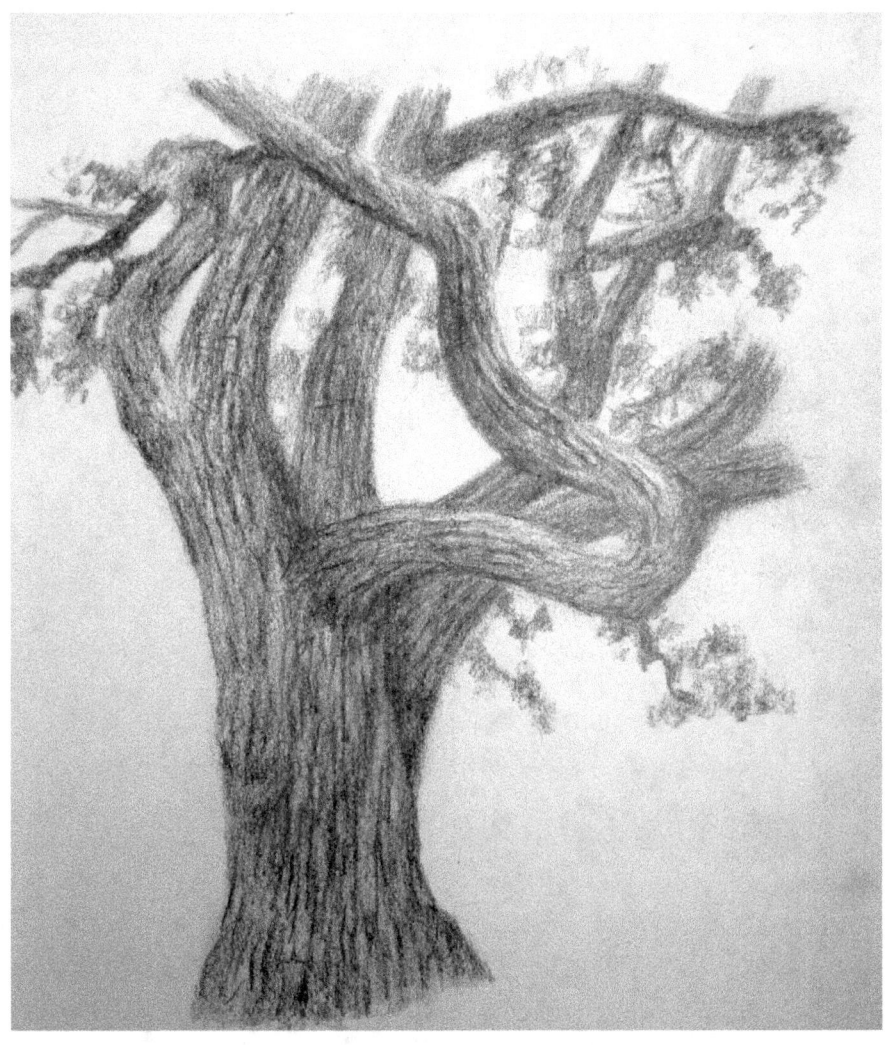

The lines in the bark of this tree were what attracted my attention to it. The deep grooves in it showed a rustic quality that I wanted to duplicate. While shading is important to capture the realism of a subject, the line quality and emphasis of details comes into play to create a finished drawing.

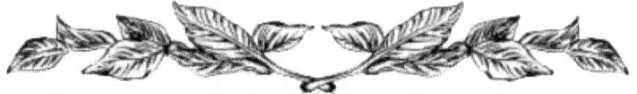

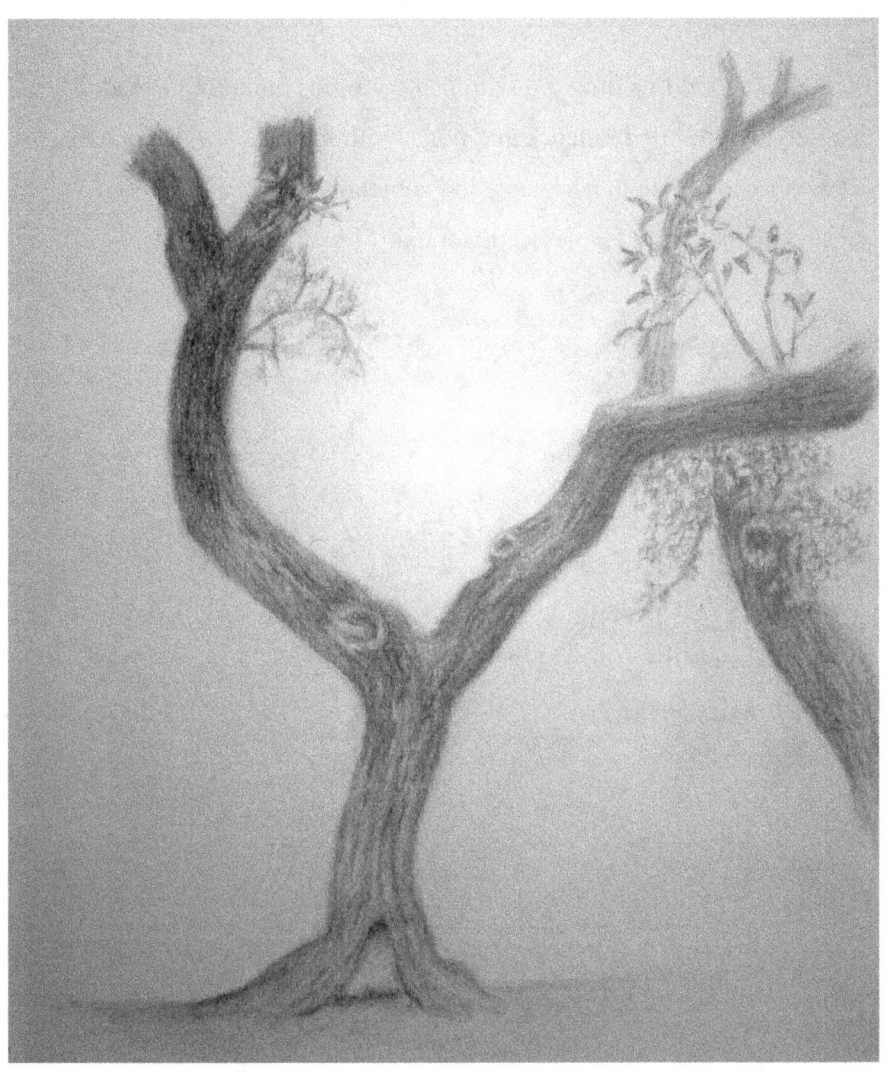

I could have left this drawing with just the limbs on it but instead, I decided to add little branches and twigs with foliage. These elements seemed to complete the drawing and somehow to add a sense of sensitivity that would have been lacking if I had left it out.

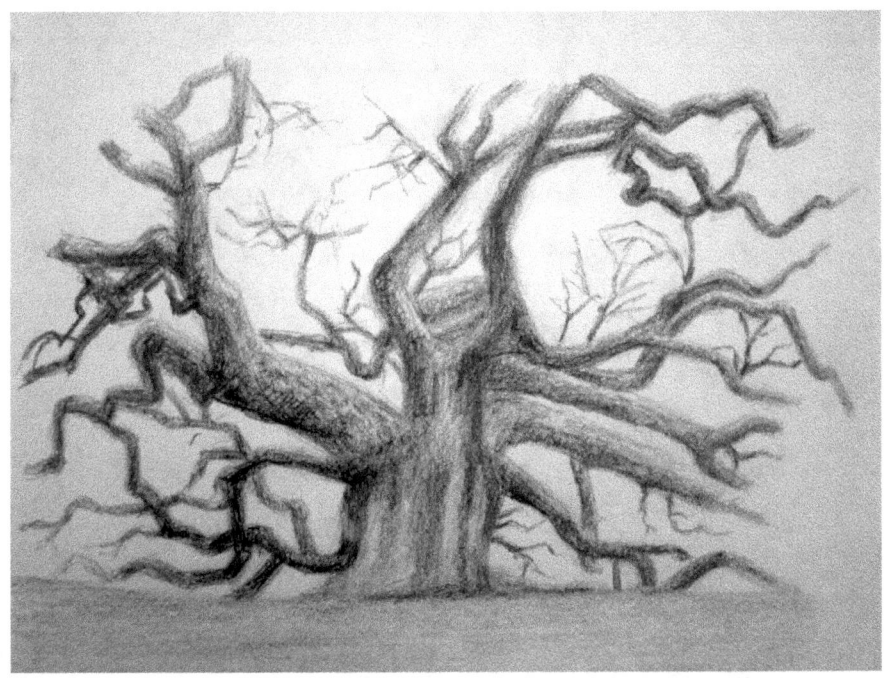

The branches in this drawing went off into many different directions and angles. Each of these limbs went off to reach the sky and find sunlight. The girth of the trunk was huge and was needed to contain all of the various branches that projected out of it. In appearance this tree was almost like a spider and yet it exhibited a sense of strength that could not be ignored.

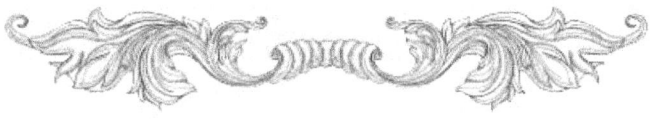

DESIGNS

Sometimes one is interested in the designs that can be formed with branches and the overall structure of a tree. This chapter is devoted to those types of drawings. Branches and limbs can overlap and form geometric patterns that sometimes are seen as symmetrical, while at other times, they are organic in nature.

After drawing so many different types of trees and their expressions, one is able to compose a drawing that is inspired from the original structure and then ad-living features in it that will compose a design rather than its natural form.

There are endless possibilities that one can draw in this manner. As each snowflake is individual in its own right, so each of these designs that I have draw here are unique.

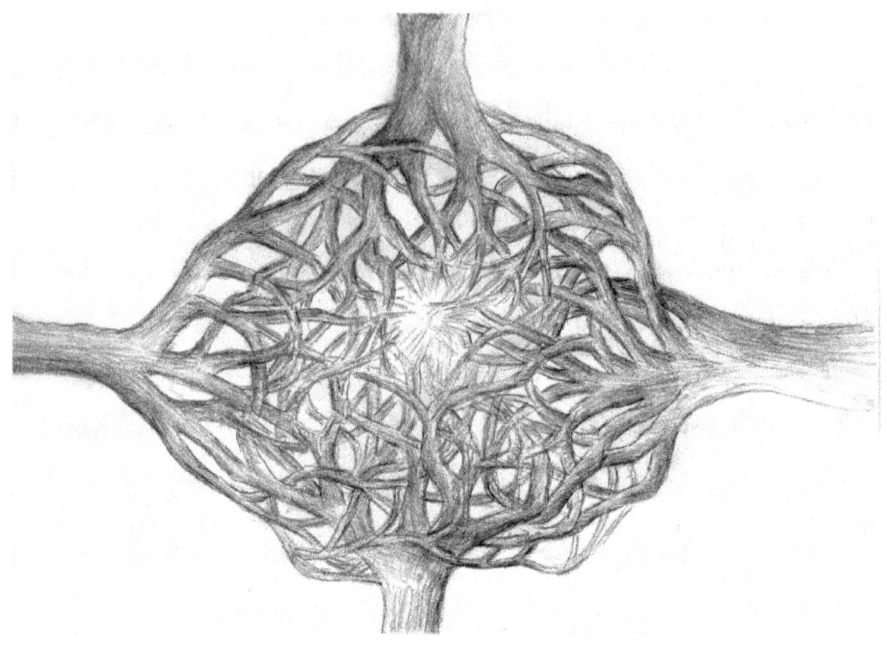

This is the first design in this section that I have drawn of trees. Everything revolves around a center point where light is reflecting back. As we know, 'God is light and there is no darkness in Him.' Light is the source of all good things in this world. The trees reach towards the heavens in search for light, and so I thought the center focus of this drawing should be one of light.

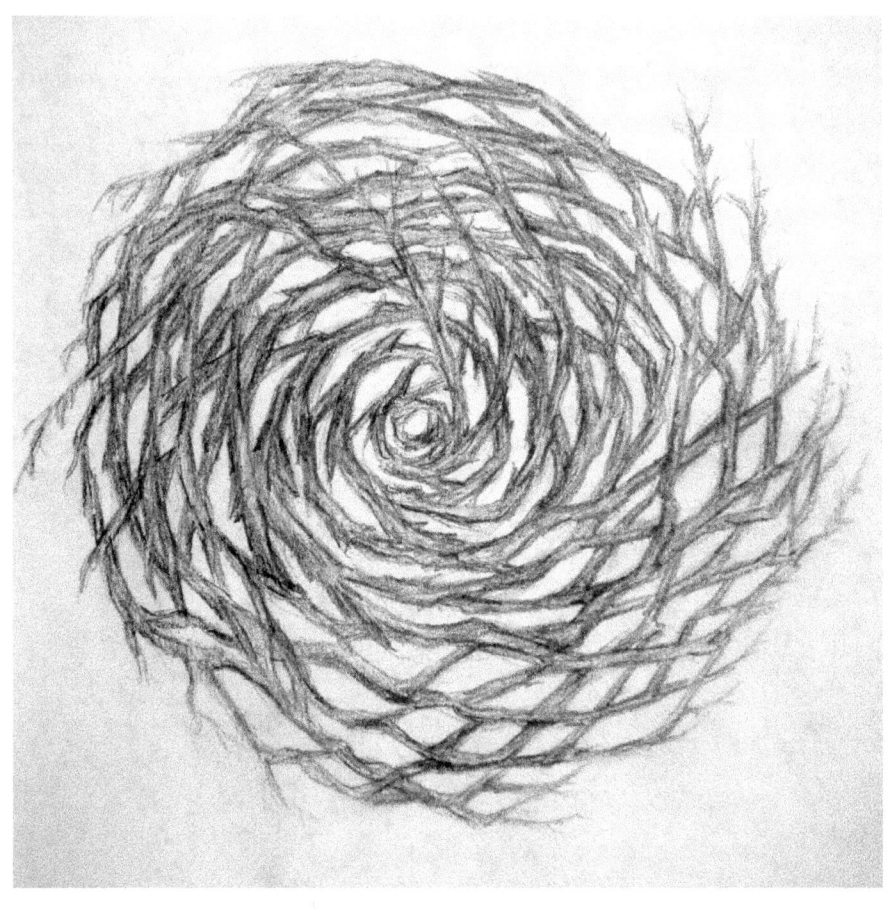

This is a spiraling type of design that shows branches revolving around a center point. Even though the shapes of the branches are somewhat rough in appearance, they still have a pattern and design that is orderly. Everything in the universe is done out of an orderly design. It is only through man that chaos has come.

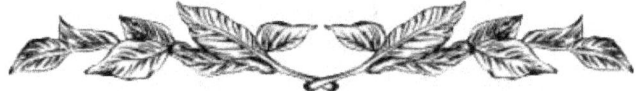

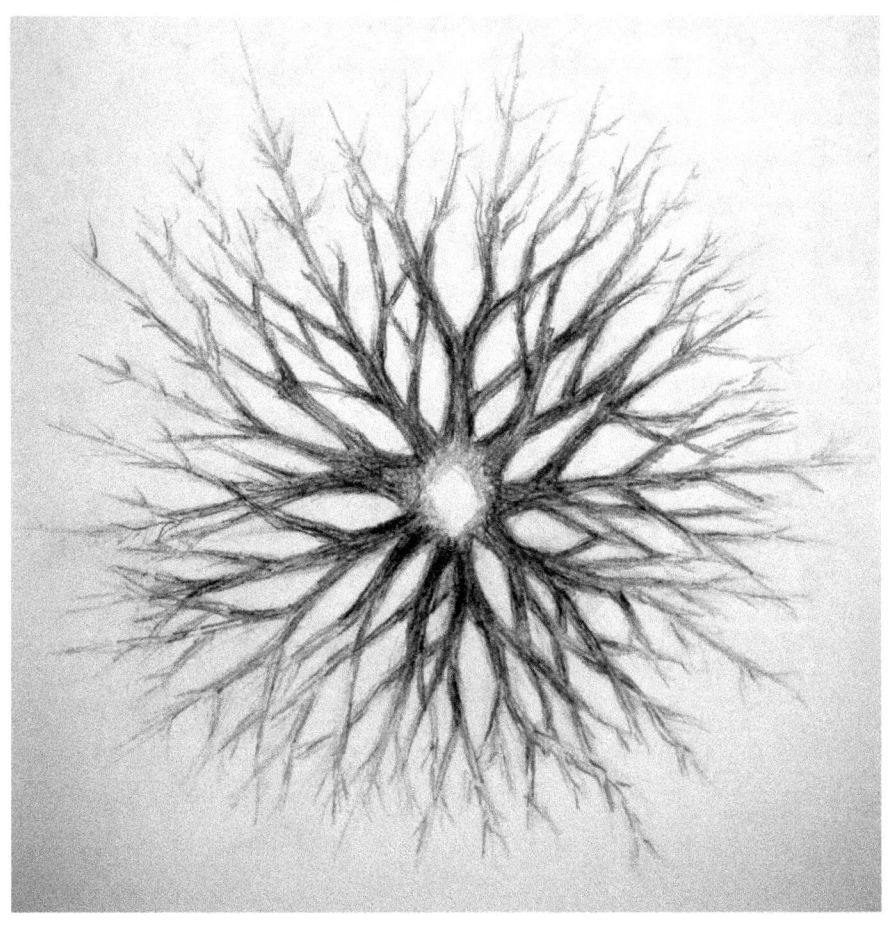

Again this previous design may appear to look in appearance with its thorny edges and shapes. And yet again, there is a symmetry that is seen that projects all of nature in it. For even the roughest and seemingly crude looking tree, has a sense of beauty in its form and design.

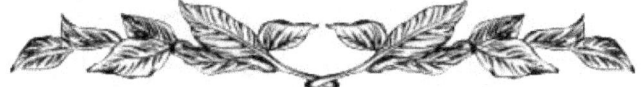

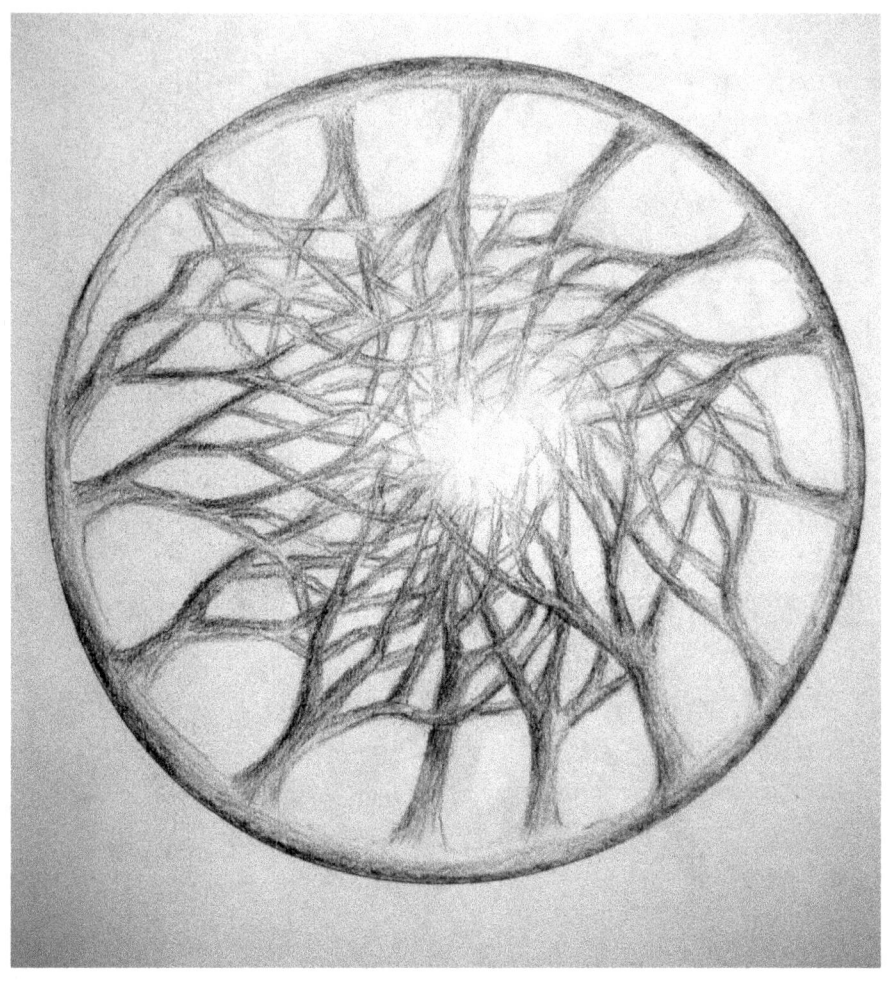

This time the pattern is circular in appearance. The trees and branches reach towards a center point rather than outwards. And yet still, there is a light at the center of the design, showing us that these forms need the light for nourishment and life. The artist can play around with many different types of designs and forms, choosing the one that seems to fit his or her desires.

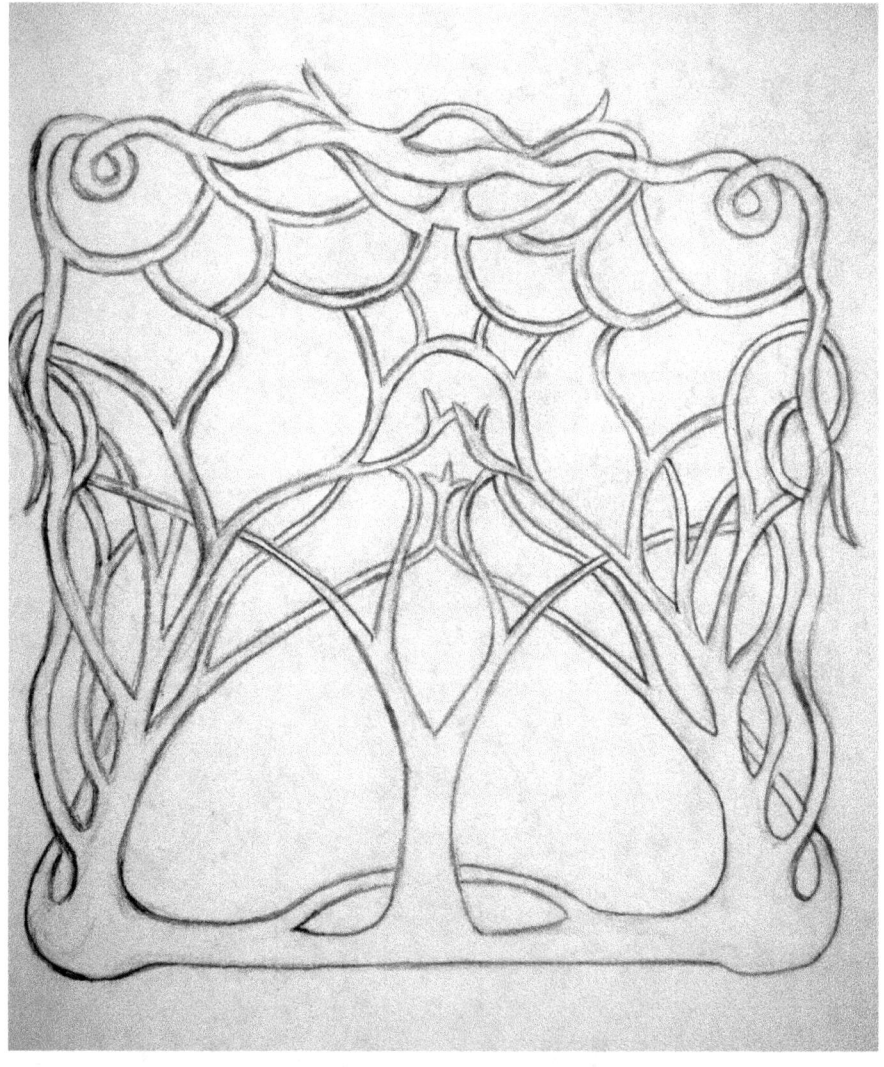

This previous design could perhaps be seen in a story book of some kind. For the shapes and lines of the drawing fit an illustration of a fantasy novel or book. I am reminded by some of the designs that can be seen in Tolkien's "Lord of the Rings." Perhaps some might remember when the Fellowship of the Ring Company came to the door at Moria. Gandalf attempted to find the words that would open the door. And finally after trying many times, he finally realized the words: 'Open Friend.'

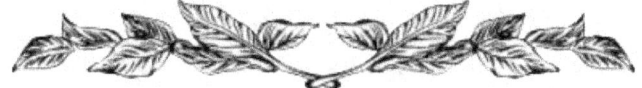

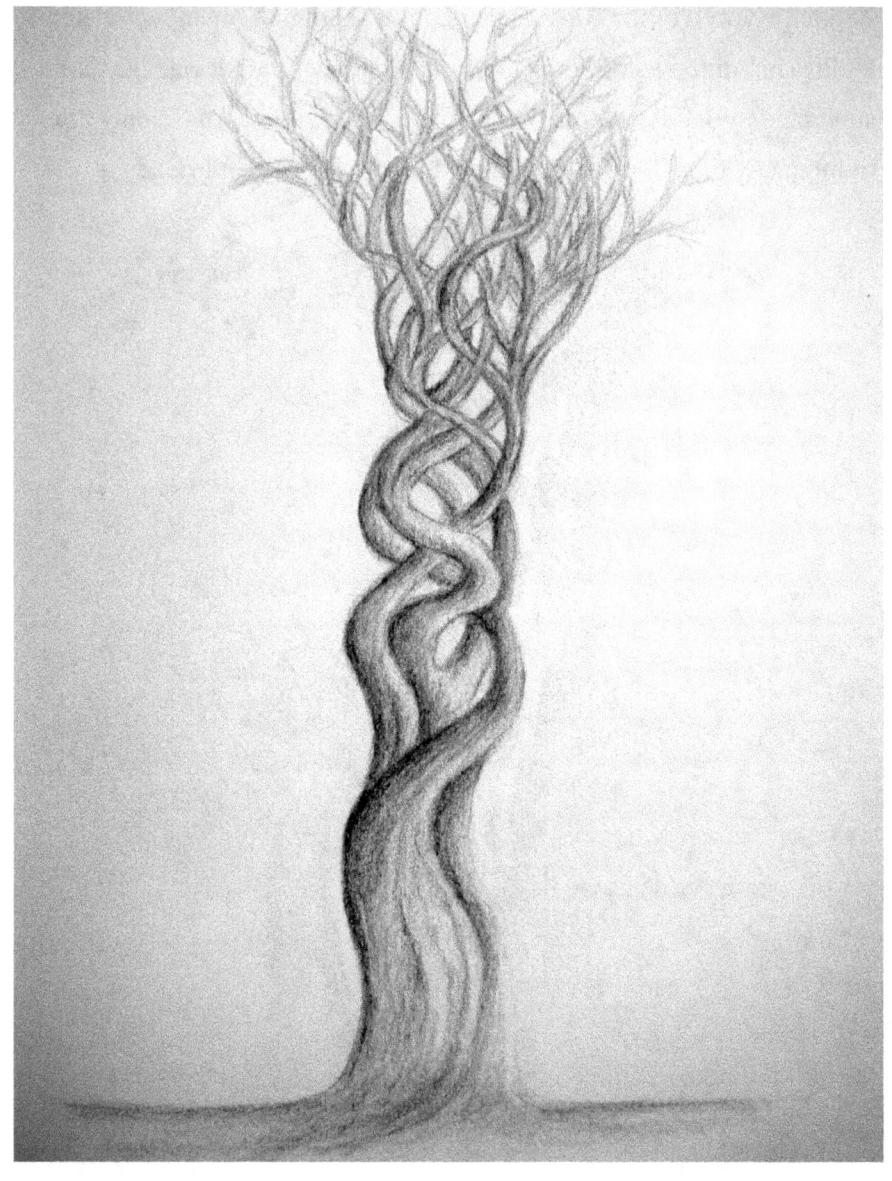

The twisting and writhing shapes of this drawing move upwards towards its center. Even as hair can be braided so also one may see limbs and branches that are also braided as the wood interlocks and twists back-in-forth. All of nature forms a pattern within itself if we would be see it in its beauty.

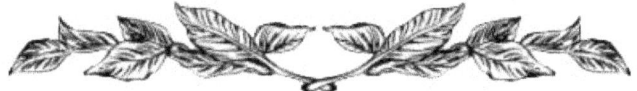

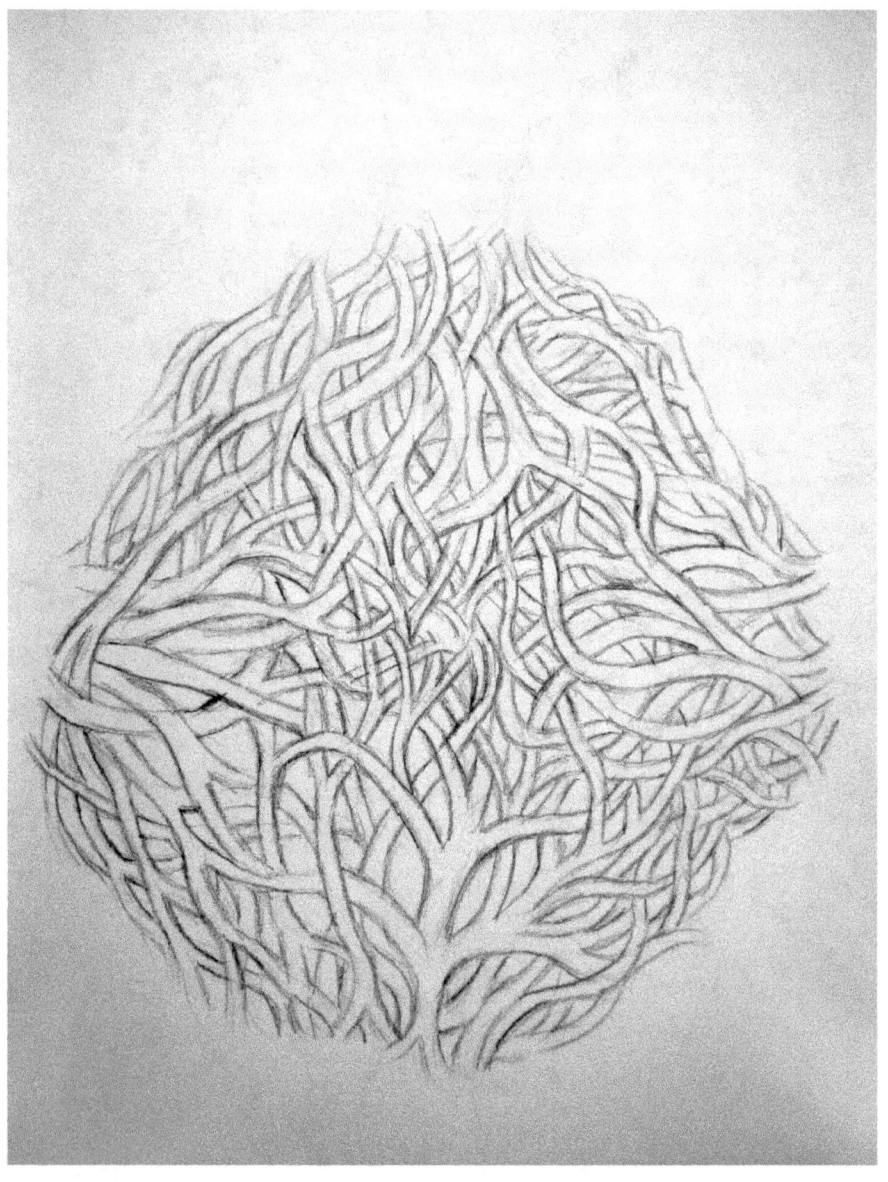

Here an elaborate pattern is formed as the flattened shapes interlock with each other. I am reminded by the complicated designs of the Celts as they created metal works and other artistic images, using rope-like patterns that are complex as well as things of incredible beauty. Many ancient cultures from the past employed designs that may well have been inspired by nature, and yet each craftsman or artisan forms his own interpretation from these inspirations.

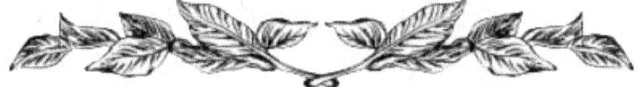

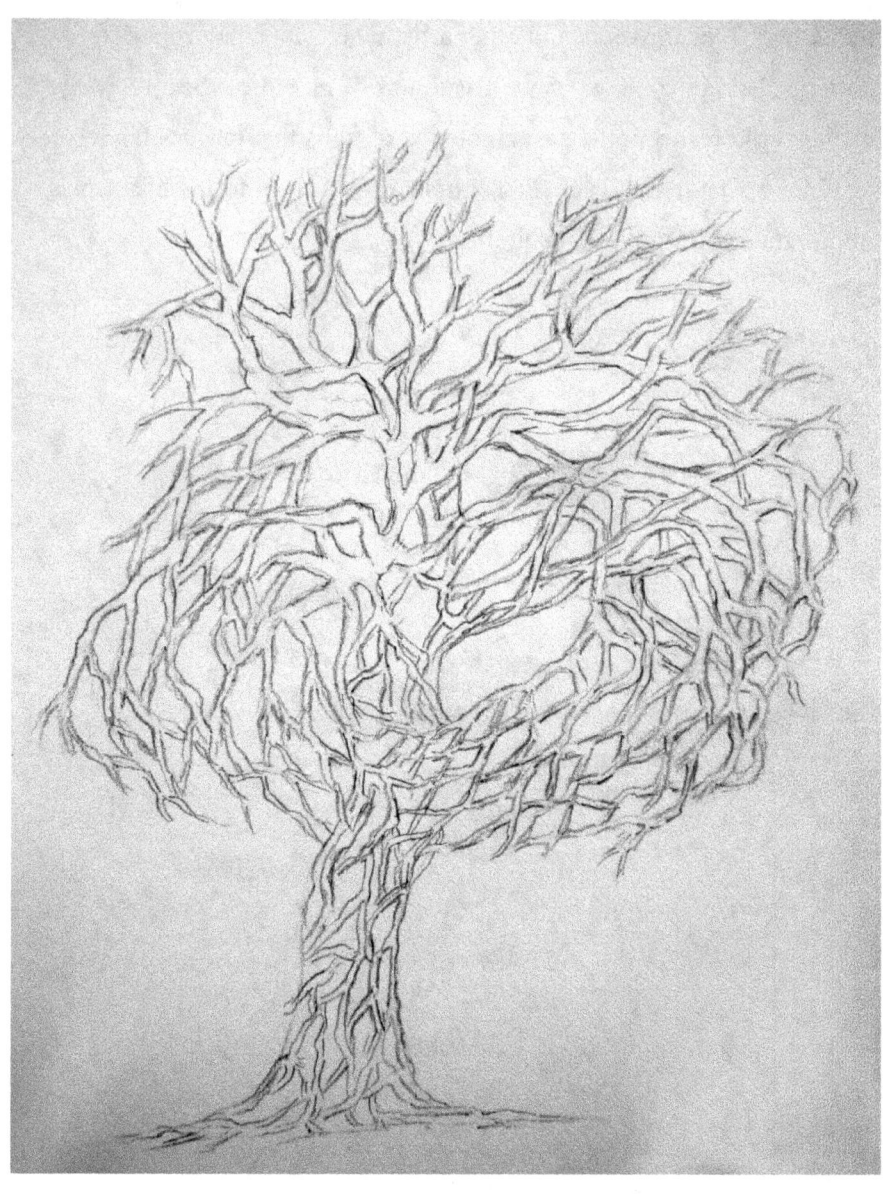

This time I chose to create interlocking patterns within each of the branches and trunk of the tree. Sometimes as seen in nature, the branches of a tree form very detailed lacy images as the twigs criss-cross with each other. It's almost like a very elaborate spider web because of the minute complexity that is seen. Take the time to notice these things in nature, and you may well see things that you haven't seen before.

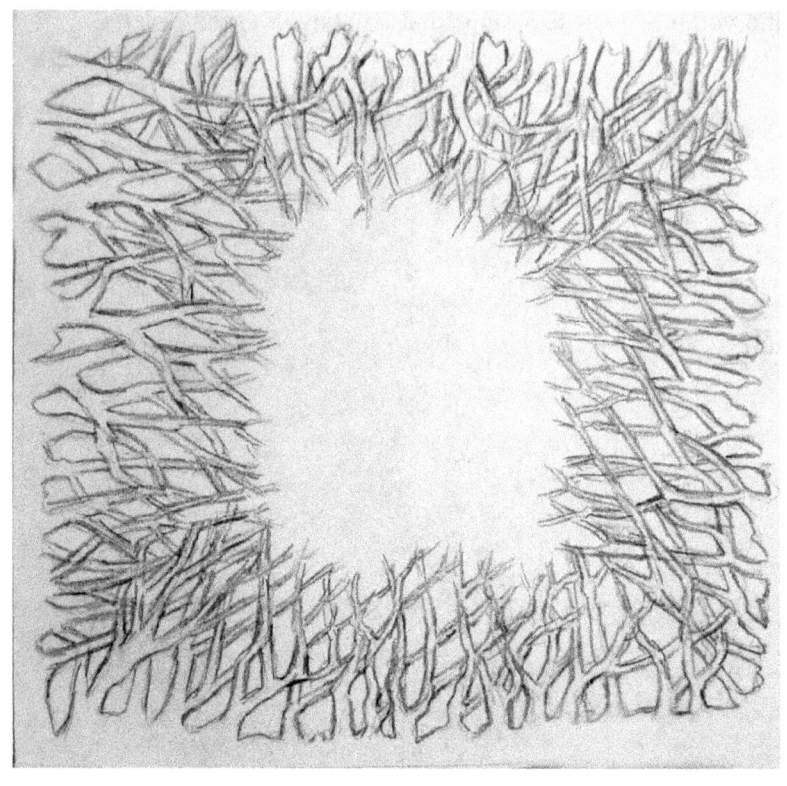

Again branches are seen as they reach inwards towards a center point. The opening is larger this time, allowing for a wider range of these elements to find their way to their nourishment. The opening in this drawing also allows the artist to break up the space thus, allowing a sense of movement or give-and-take, to be seen in it.

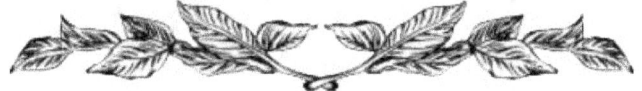

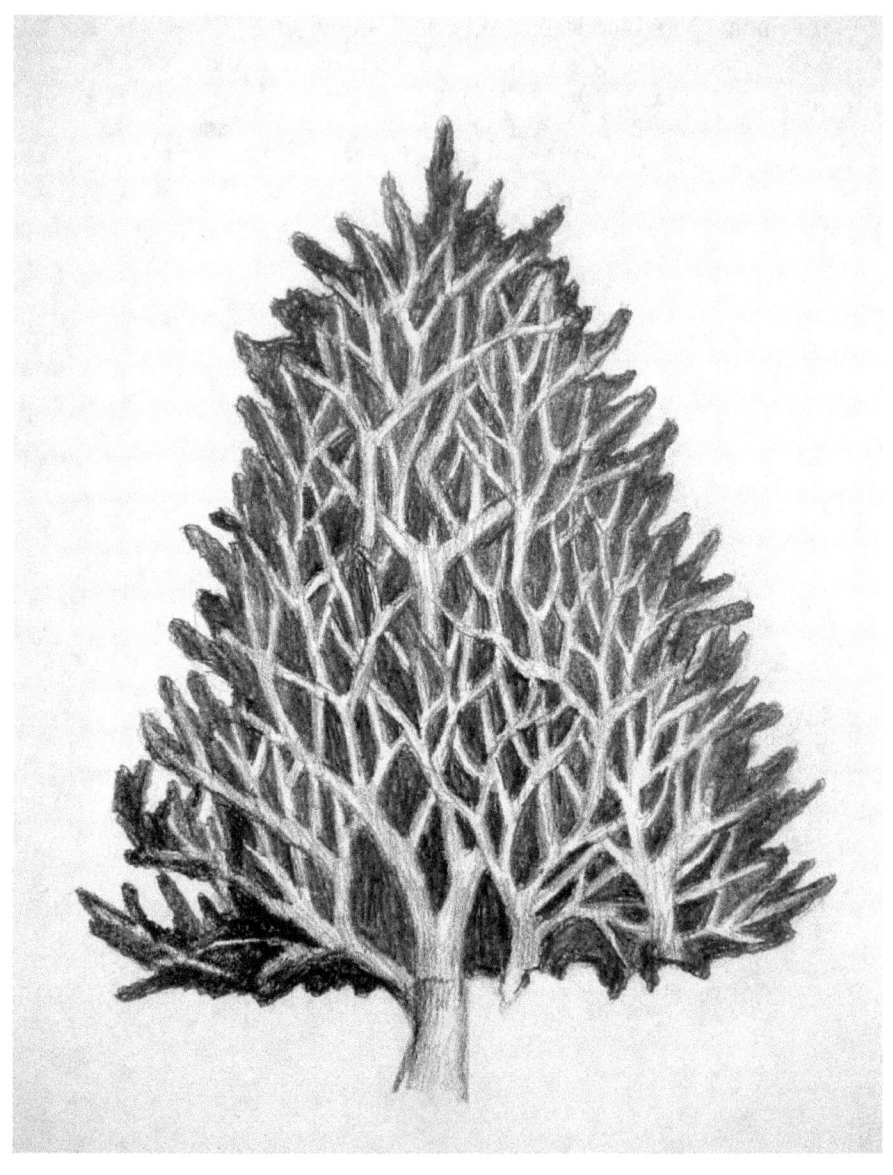

This time I decided to do a drawing of a simple Christmas-type of shape for the tree. And now within the boundaries there are branch-like shapes on the inside of it. Certainly there are branches to be found within the evergreen branches of a Christmas tree, but the details that are here, are perhaps more detailed and barren in origin.

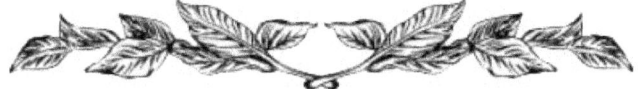

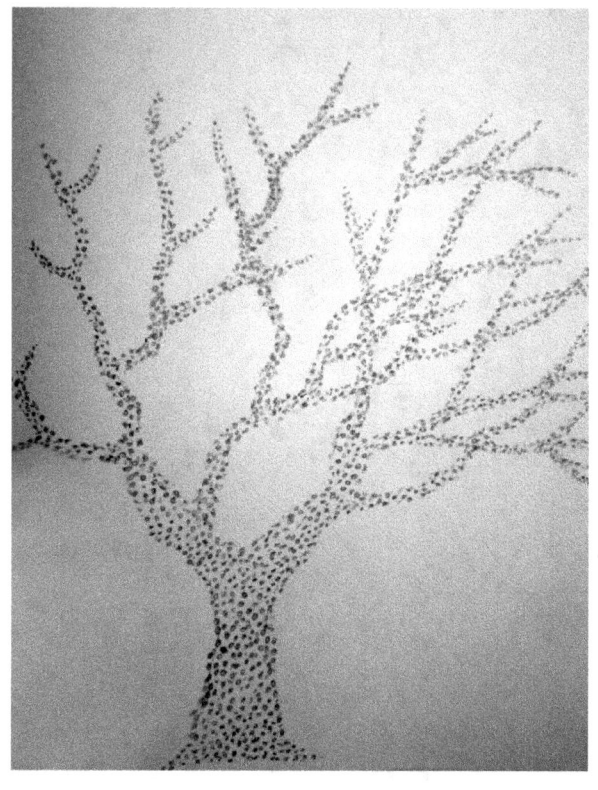

All types of drawing strokes can be used to create a design. One can use lines, cross-hatching, or in this case dots. Every one of the branches and trunk are filled full of these dots. These types of markings can be decorative or they can be simply a shape of some sort. Either way a design should be part of the overall drawing and illustrate a sense of unity in it.

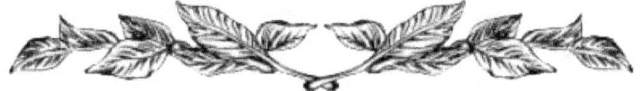

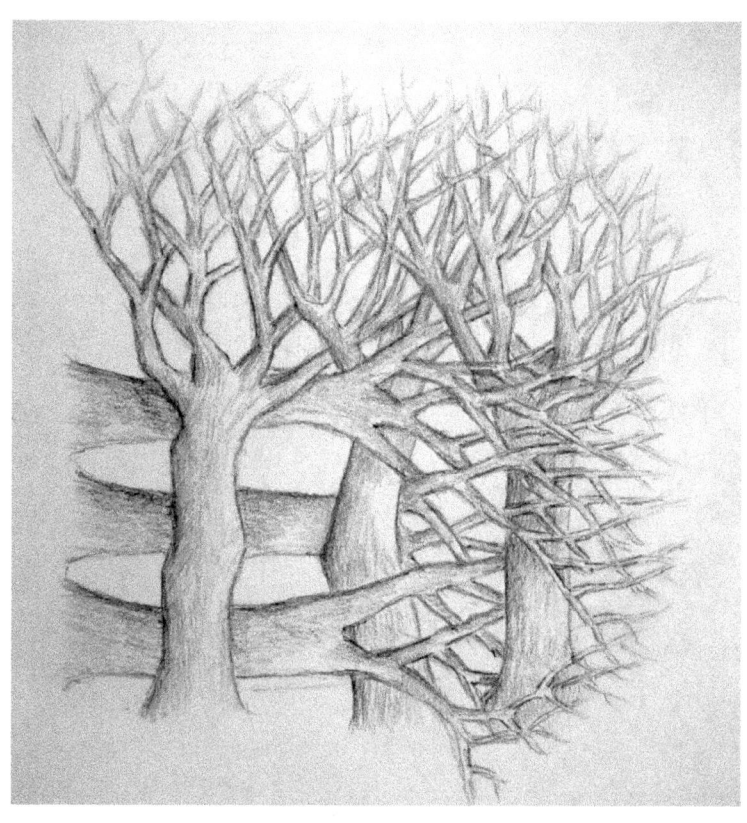

I wanted to 'shift' some of the trees this time on one angle and then transpose them another way. One can view this drawing different ways as each angle of the trees plays against the other one. It's almost like one hand in each section of the trees is seen one way, and then if you turn the drawing, one can see the section. Perhaps one can be reminded of the incredible work of M.C. Escher, although my work can't be compared to his.

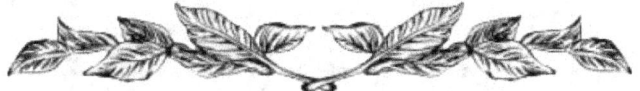

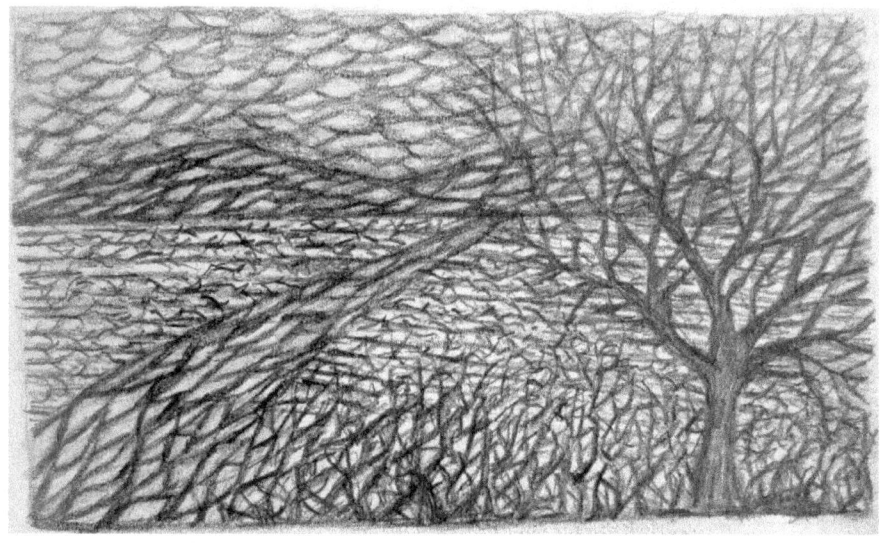

A drawing can take on the form and texture of various things. In this case I wanted to create different sections that somehow took on the look of an old piece of carpet. The artist can begin using a certain technique and line quality to depict something, and then change it in a different place. But all-in-all a piece of artwork should reflect a sense of unity in it as a whole.

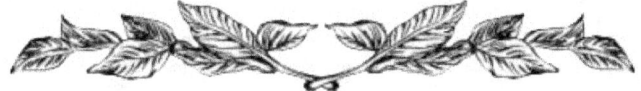

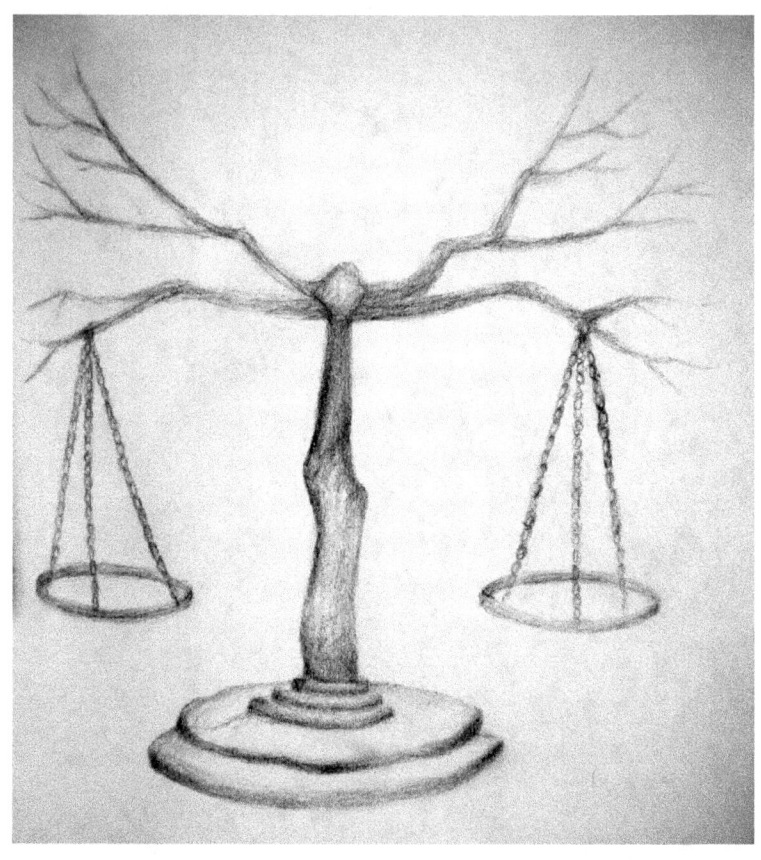

The whole concept of balance has always intrigued me, especially in how things can be equalized as the weight on both sides become level with each other.

A balance beam is often identified with the concept of justice. I wanted to simply take the center post of the balancing beam and extend into the branches of a tree.

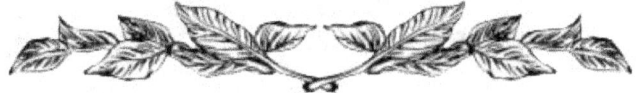

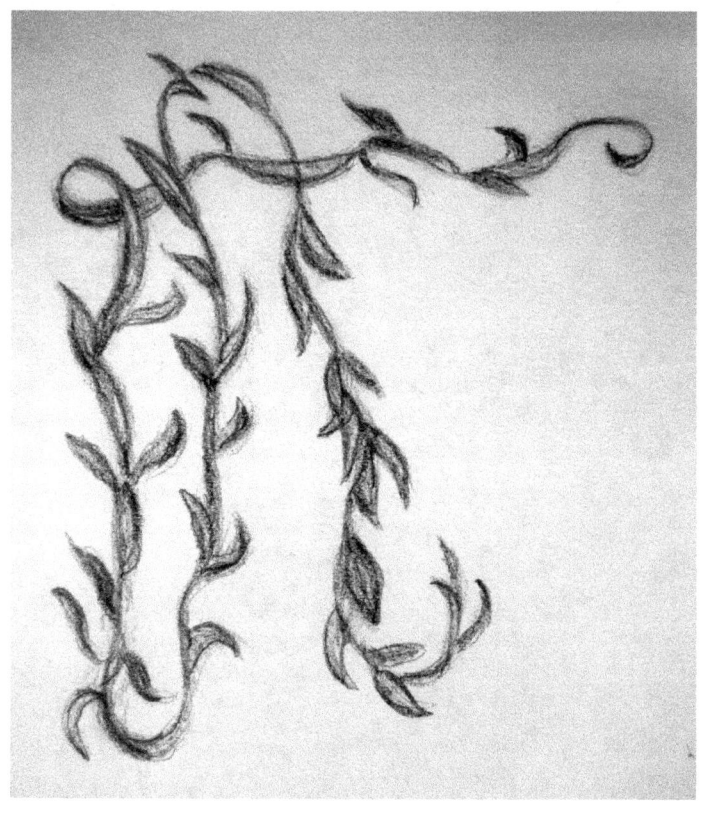

The forms of leaves and vines have always inspired me, especially how they curve and wrap around the spaces they are in. One sees vines as they wrap around a fence, a pillar, or a window. The great illustrator, designer and artist William Morris, used leaf forms and other images to adorn his many elaborate designs and tiles.

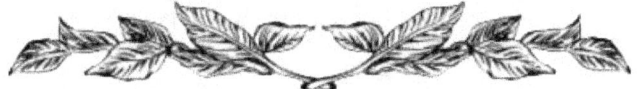

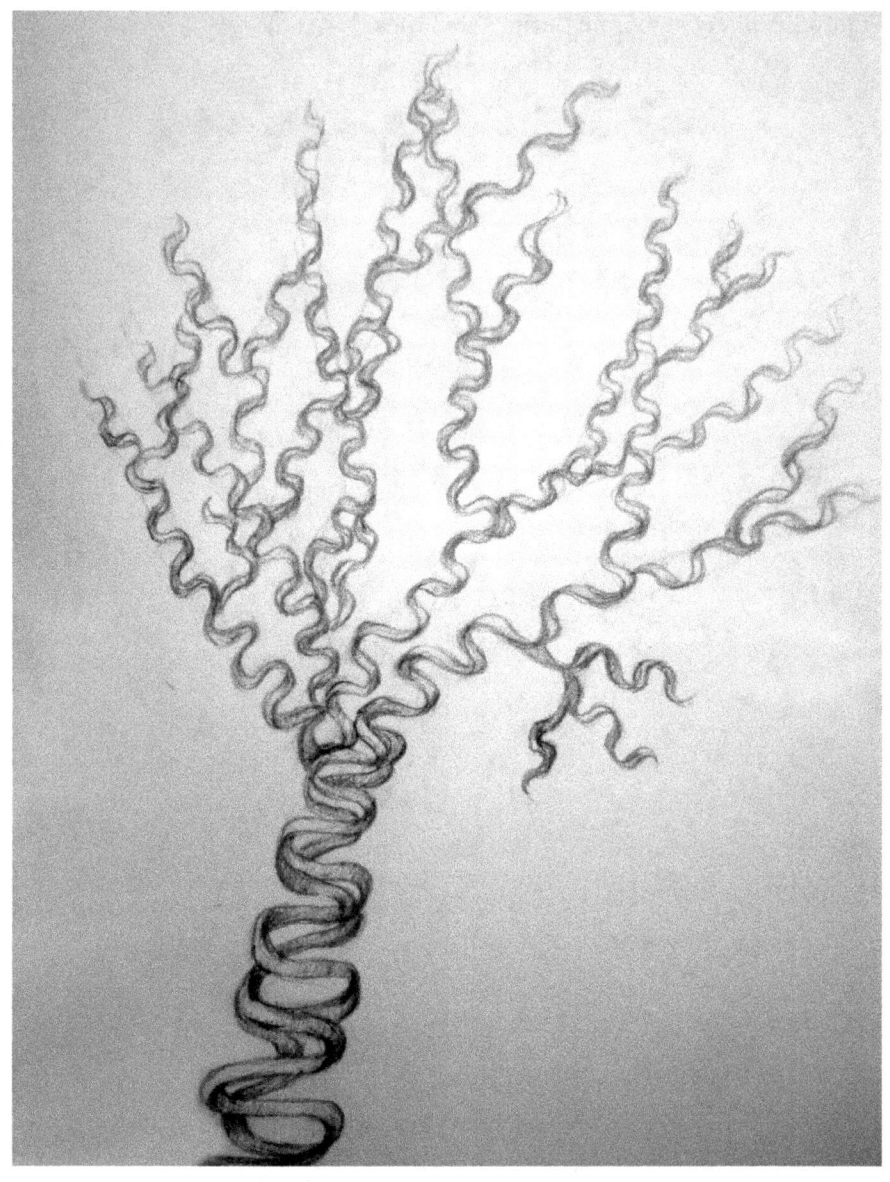

Years ago I remember seeing some of Salvador Dali's paintings and had seen how he had used the shape of ribbons to create the form of a face. I wanted to try the same thing in this drawing, where the ribbons wrap around the circumference of the limbs and branches.

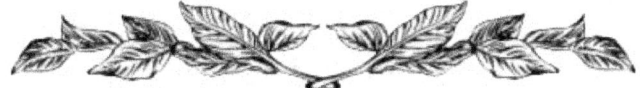

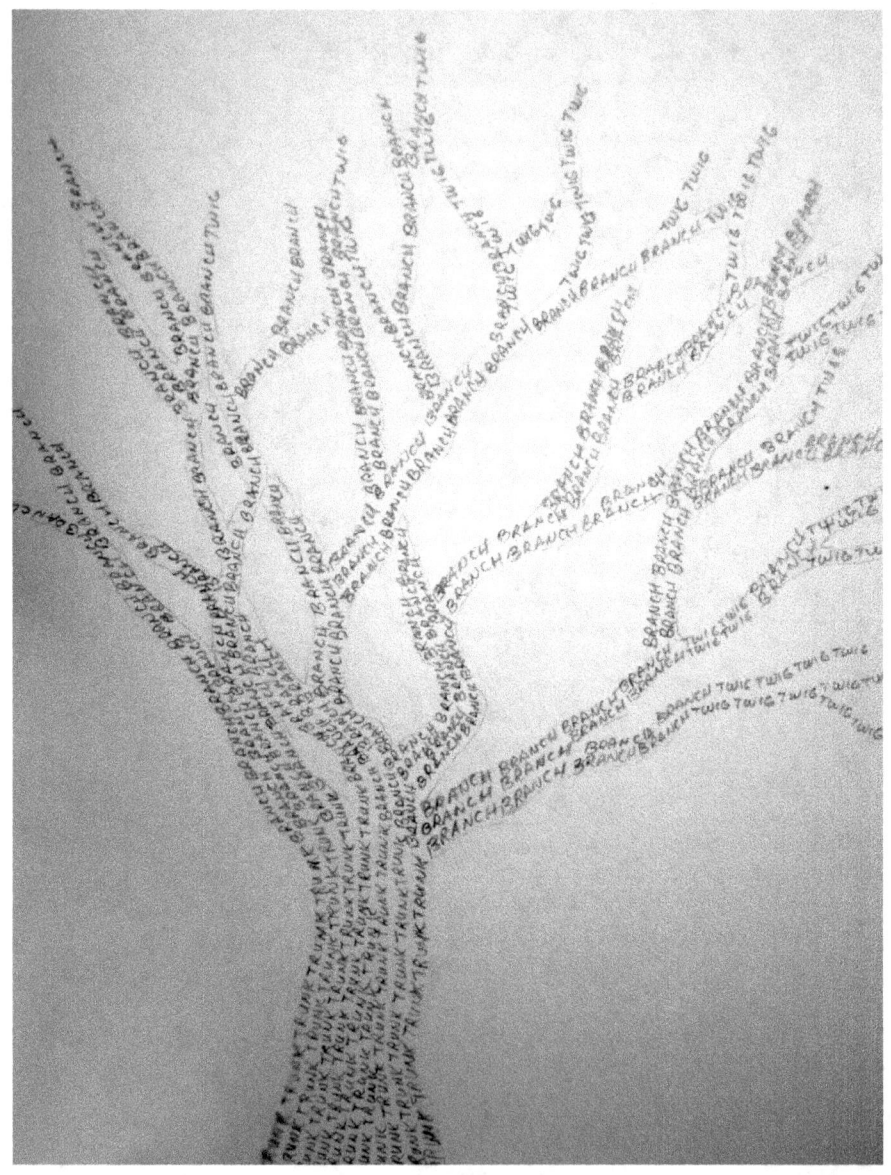

One may not realize it but the artist can use all types of things to enclose or make-up a drawing. Years ago I had done a drawing of tree that included words in its form. I decided to do this again for this one. Words can almost take on the form of a script that may or may not look like words or letters, but if one looks closer they will see them.

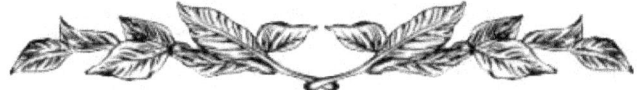

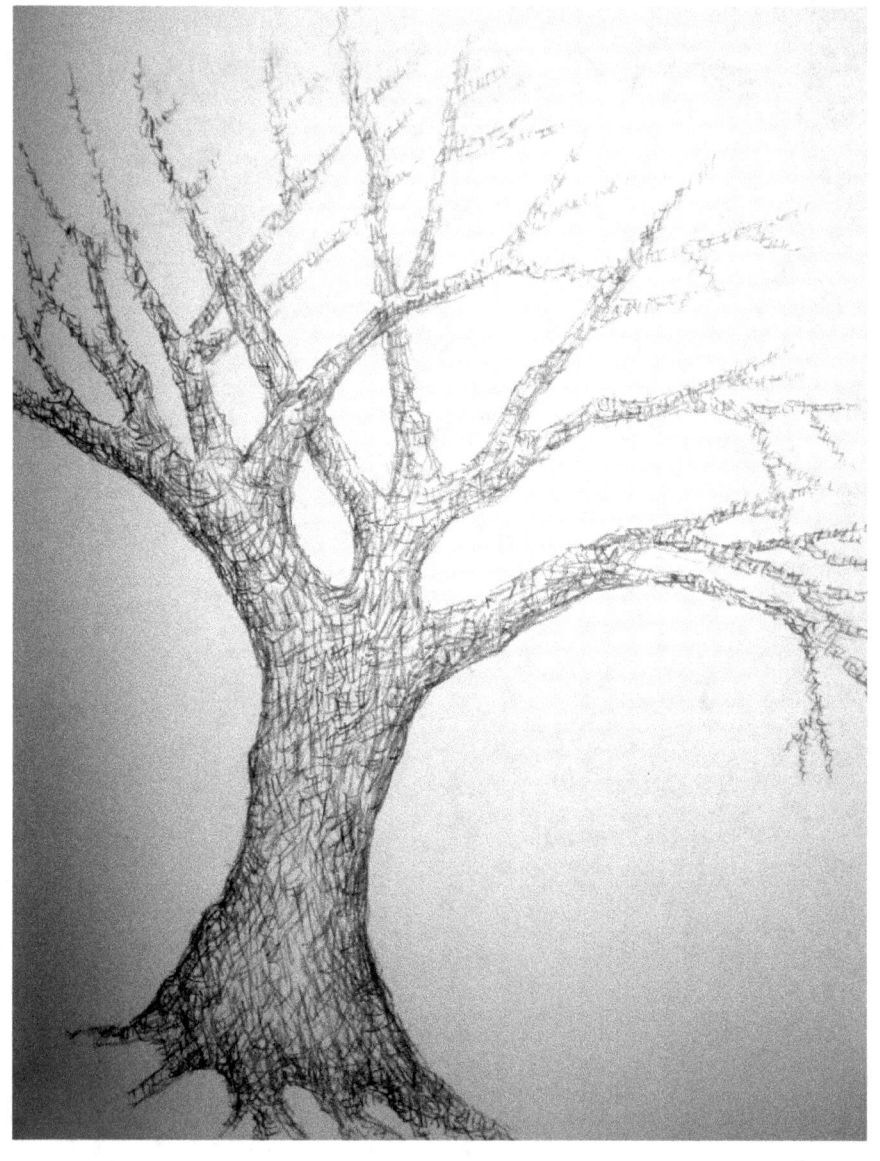

Cross-hatching is a technique that is often used in drawing. It offers the artist a way to create lines from a back-and-forth motion of intersecting lines to create volume and form.

In this previous drawing of a tree, I decided to use this technique for the drawing. I believe it captured the overall effect I wanted. One doesn't always have to use elaborate shading to do a drawing; there are many different effects that are at the artist's disposal.

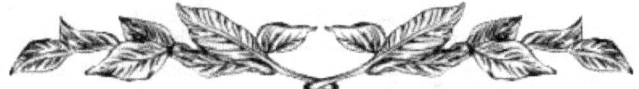

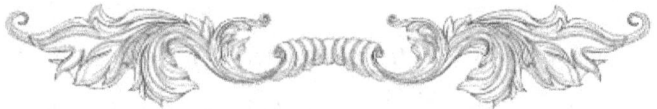

ROOTS

Just as the limbs, branches and the trunks of a tree exhibit the individual properties that are inherent in each, so there are also unusual roots that one finds at its base.

In this last section I have endeavored to show the many different types of roots that I have seen in my wanderings. Each one of them has instinctive shapes and forms in them, and as such they are a tree unto themselves.

Some of these come out of huge openings that look like caves while others simply criss-cross like snakes in their curves and lines.

I hope you enjoy looking through these examples as much as I had fun in drawing them. The drawings in this book go back over the last several years and show perhaps a history of the types of things that have inspired me over time.

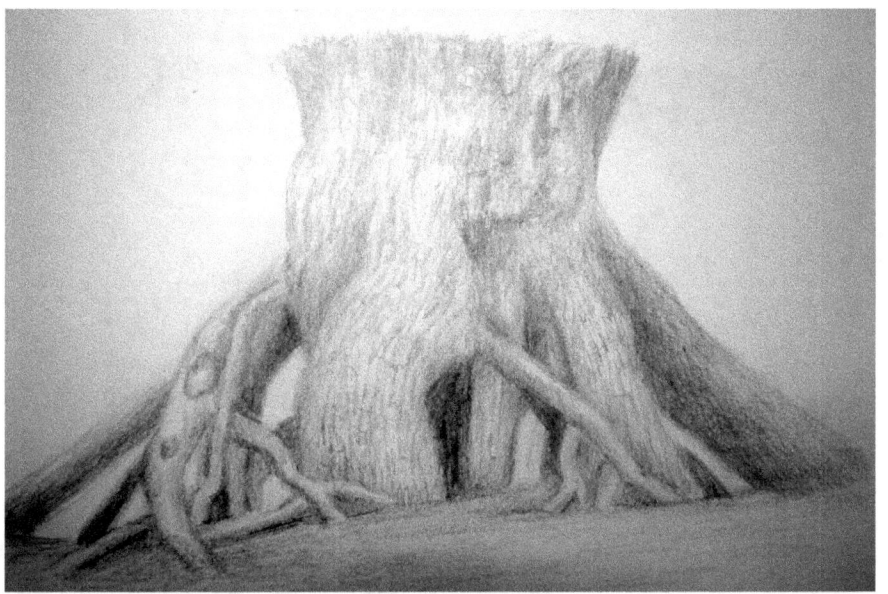

There are as many different types of roots as there are trees in this world. Each one is unique in its own way. The base of this tree has roots that spread out into uniform angles providing a strong sturdy foundation. The roots of a tree are very important for the overall sturdiness and strength of the tree. Without it, the tree would decay and wither.

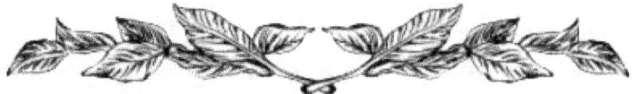

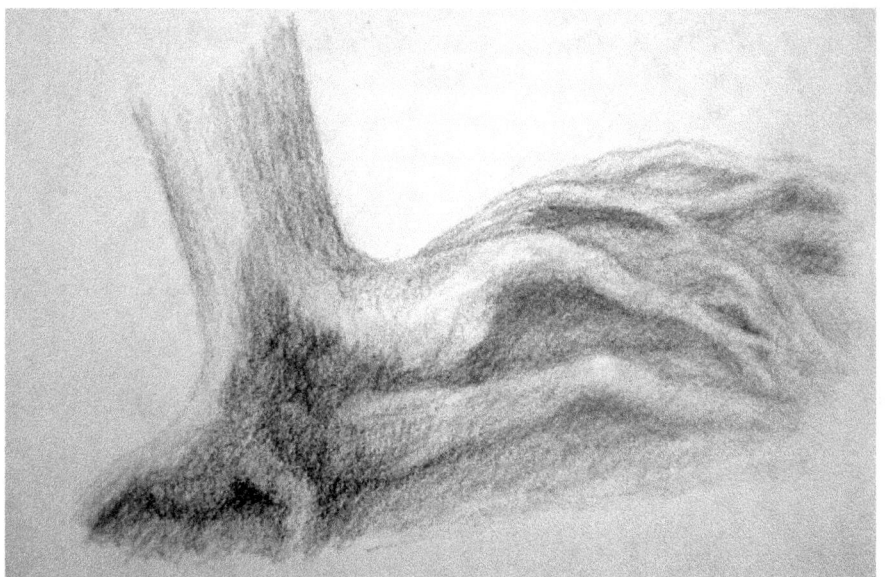

This tree is almost like a foot as it arches outwards and upwards, with the branches forming toes. The earth around the roots of a tree are crucial especially to the artist, because these spaces form negative areas which are just as important as the positive shapes that are seen around them.

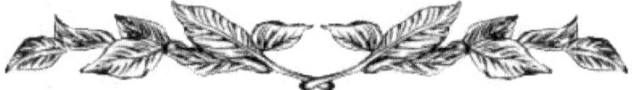

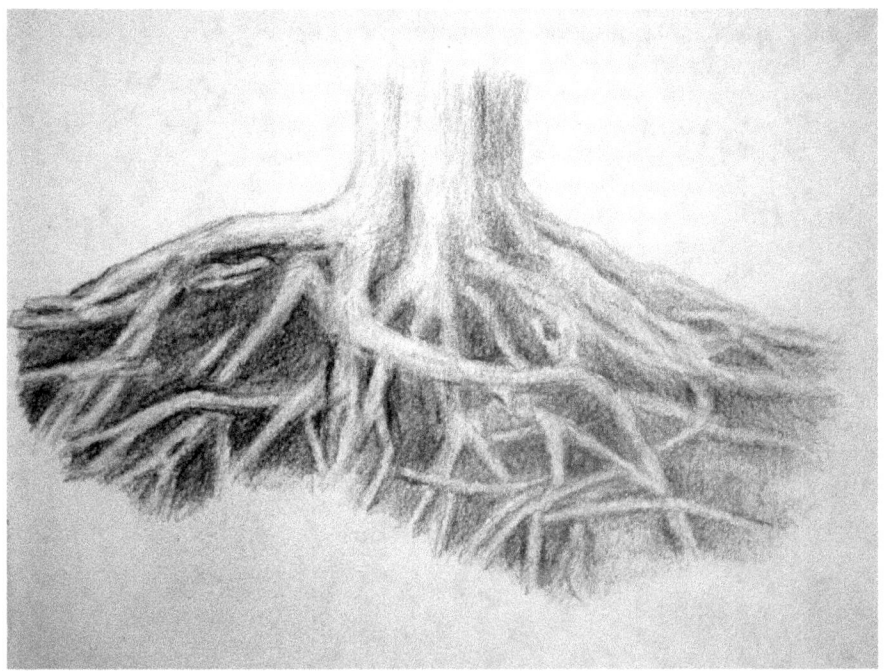

This tree had a root system that was typical in its form and display. Each and every section of the roots of a tree will spread out from its base in such a way that the tree itself will have a firm and stable foundation. As each of these roots spread out, they become smaller in circumference just like the arteries of our blood system form capillaries

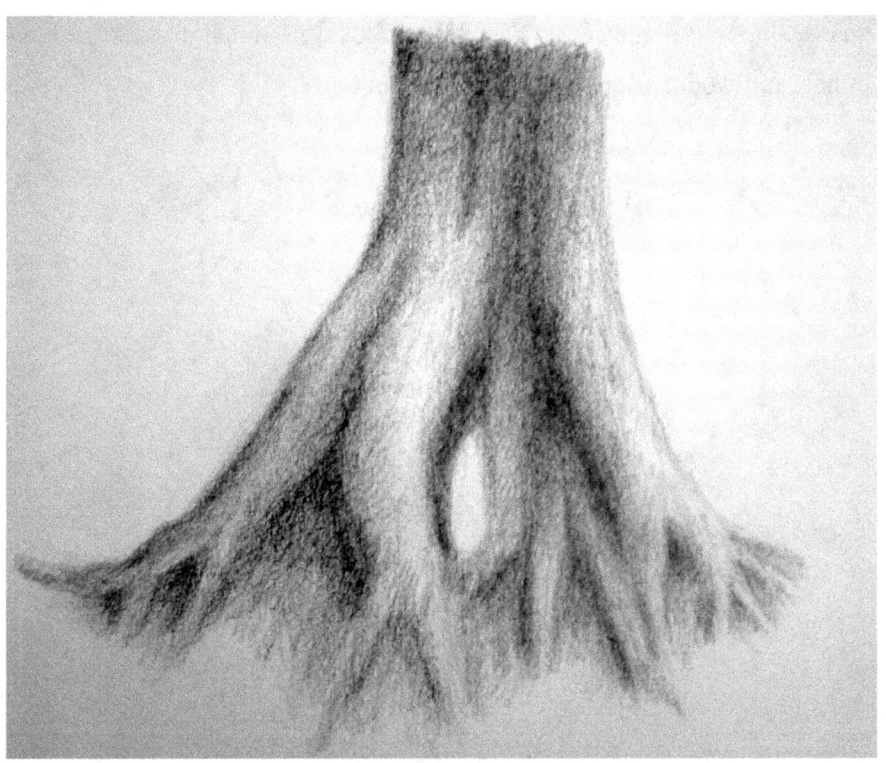

This particular root system is very simple and yet each of the sections are rather large but adequate for the entire tree. In this case, it is not a complex area as seen in other root systems. One will notice that there is an opening within the center part of this root system that divides the area in half and would allow one to peer within it.

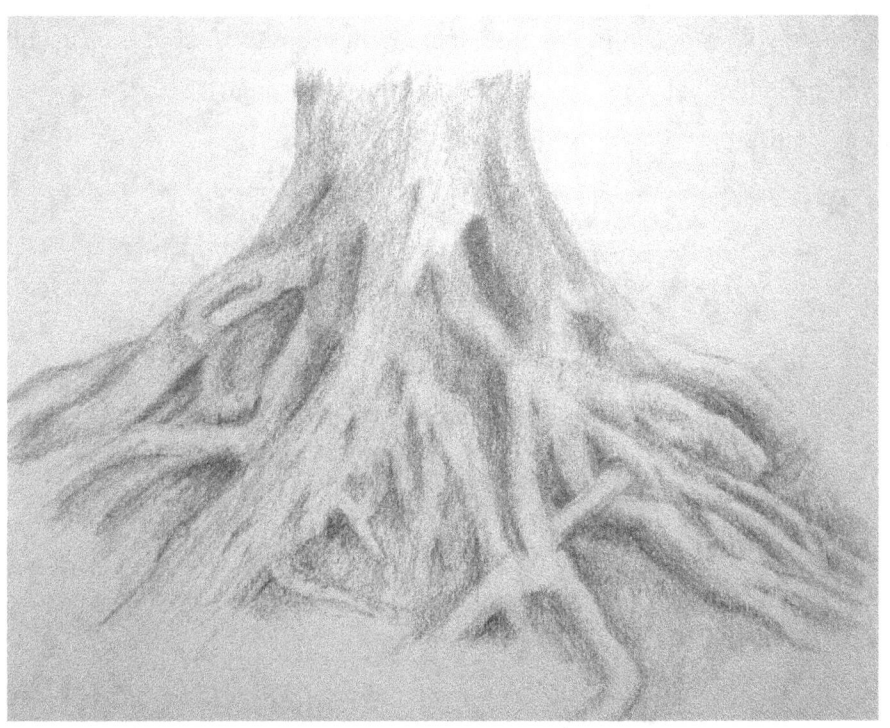

Sometimes a drawing is dark and detailed showing all of the minute parts that are within it. But in this case, there is an overall soft appearance, and yet the individual parts are still quite visible to be seen. The artist has many different styles at his disposal that he can use.

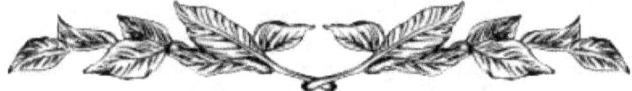

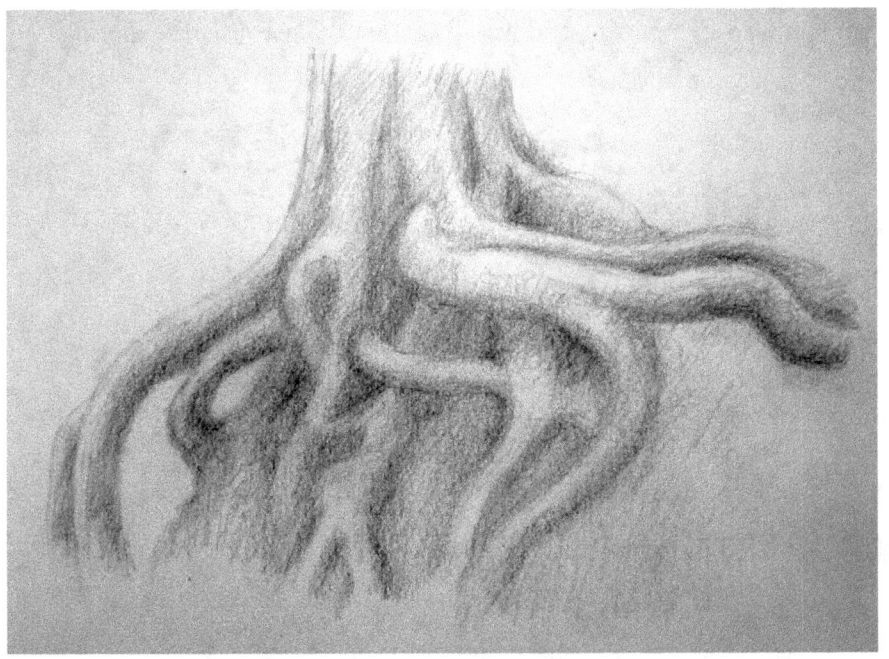

The drawing on the previous page has roots in it that are almost tubular or like an octopus in appearance. Imagination is key for the artist and one would be wise to use it. It is one thing to be able to duplicate something very realistic, and yet it is another to use artistic expression.

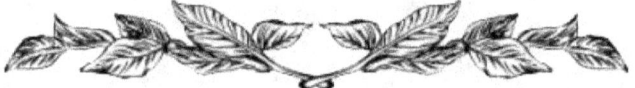

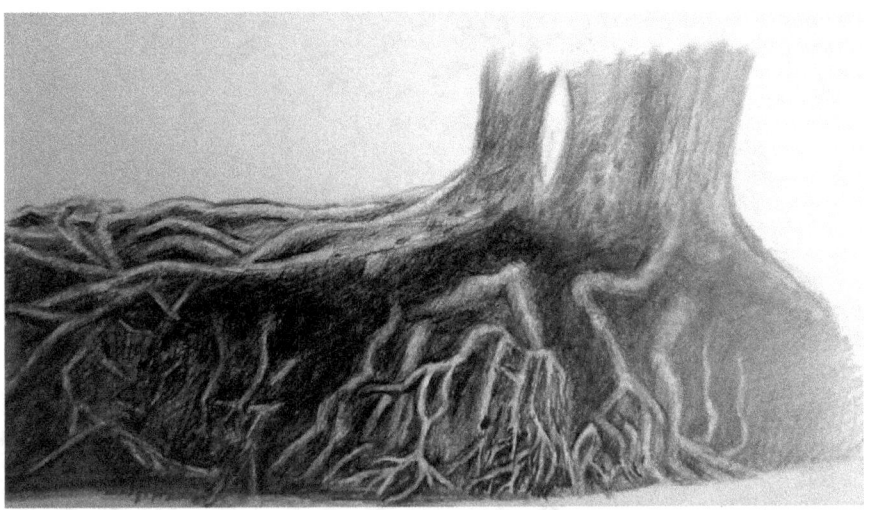

This drawing is darker, and one might even consider that the roots that are seen there could almost have been seen in a cave. The roots intertwine with each other in almost a mysterious or even an ominous way. A piece of artwork can project any number of different types of moods. Sometimes these moods are planned and at other times they just happen without thinking about them beforehand.

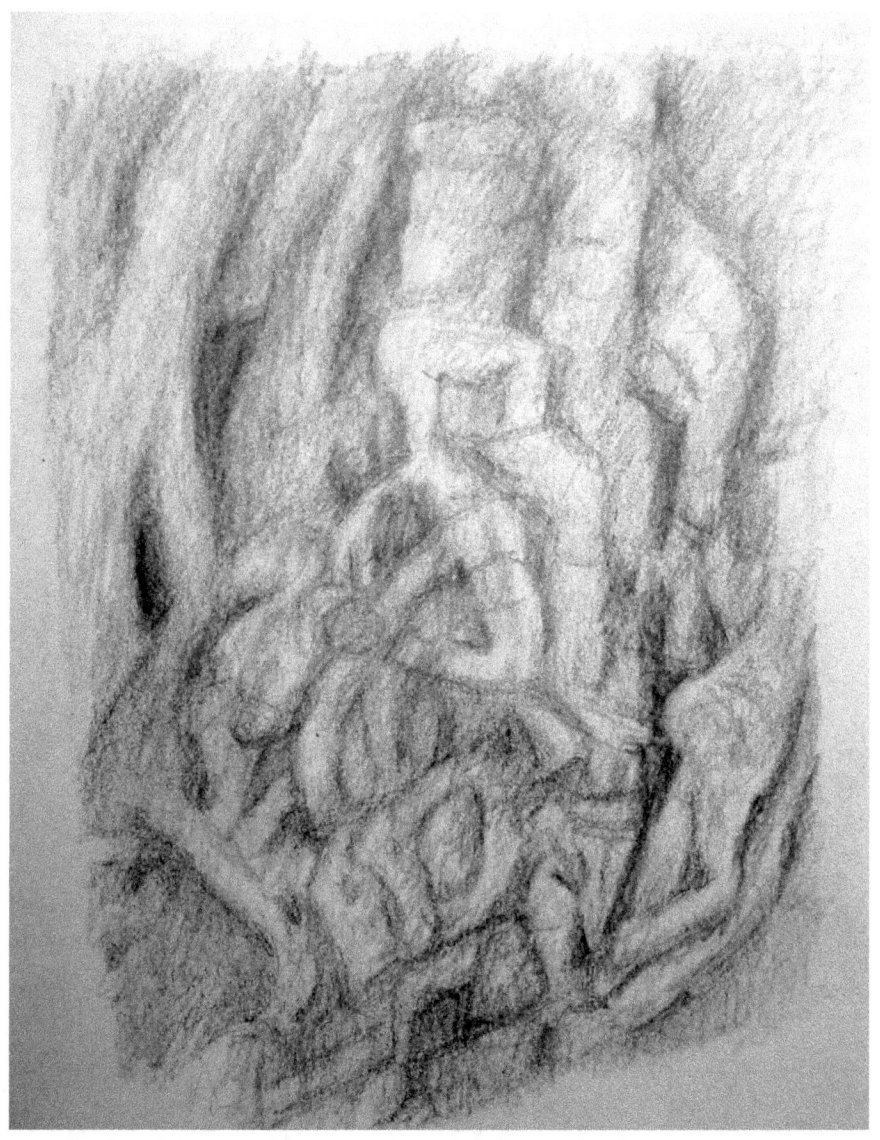

This previous drawing is in some ways almost like a sculptural relief that seems to depict various figures in it. Again, this wasn't intentional by any means. These types of things are sometimes seen because our imagination allows the viewer and the artist to see them. However, this particular scene was drawn from a section of roots and not of human figures.

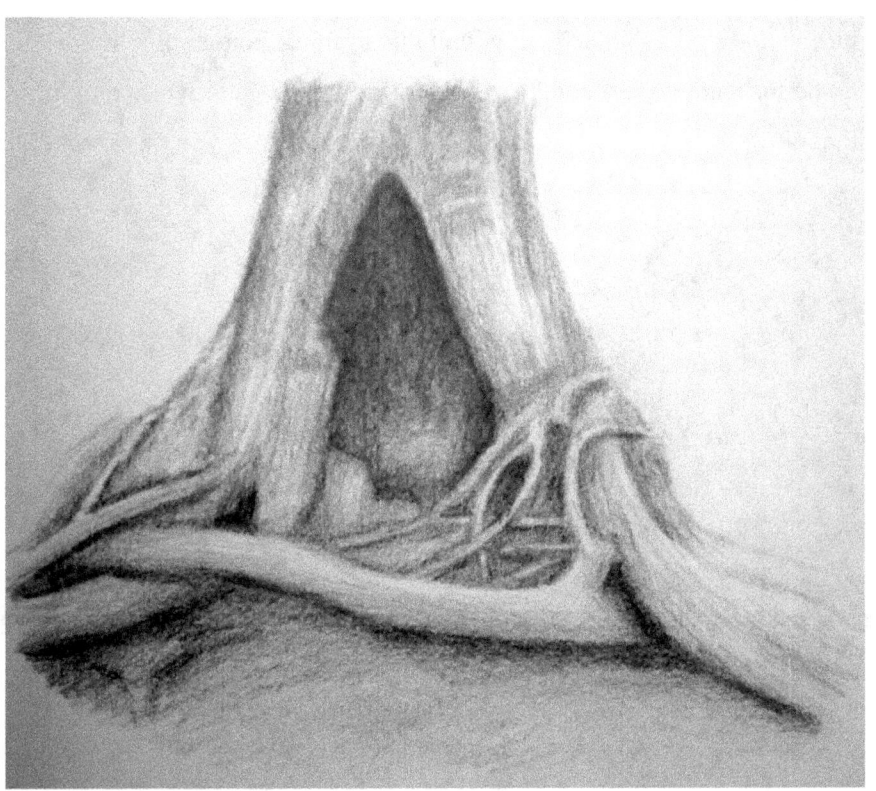

This time a cave is definitely seen as the roots themselves seem to emanate from the darkness within the tree. Perhaps a small squirrel or a bird would find its home here within this opening. Nature provides a home for many to rest and keep warmth from the winter winds and snow that blows.

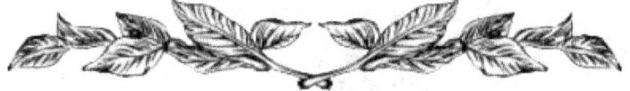

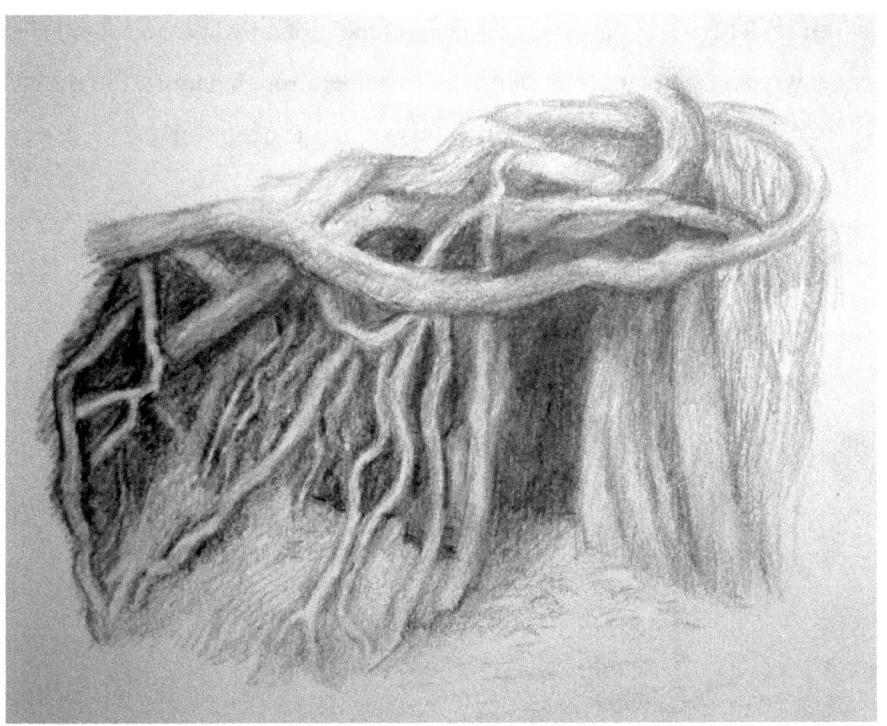

This is the very last drawing in this book. Again, the viewer will see a deep cavern beyond the roots that spread out in various directions. One larger root expands out around the edges of the cave, wrapping across the entrance. There is a sandy appearance on the ground where the smaller roots wrap around and find their way twisting through and next to each other. One might wonder what resides within the deep cavern.

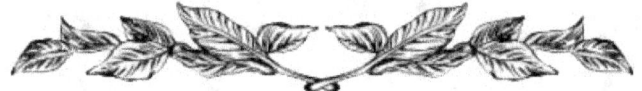

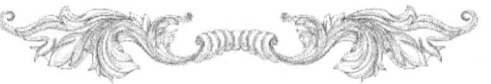

ABOUT THE AUTHOR

Stephen grew up in Lindsborg, Kansas and spent his time observing the many things around him that a small town could offer. He grew up going to high school and college in Lindsborg at Bethany College, graduating in 1978 with B.A in art. During his late high school and early college years, he spent time developing his style, studying all of the various artists throughout history. He often went and visited the late Lester Raymer, a well-known artist who died in the 1980's. He remembers the times that people would often come to visit Lester, and he would pull the curtains shut because he would rather not talk with the public.

Stephen spent twenty-one years teaching high school art in Colorado Springs, and because of the budget cuts in many schools throughout the nation, he found himself looking for other employment. He decided that now was a good time to devote to his art and to pursue it more seriously. Over the last few years he has packed up his French easel and headed for the nearby canyons and mountains to paint. There are so many different scenes and places that one could paint here. With the changing of the seasons, there are new and different palettes to use, and inspirations to find.

He believes that the artist sees the world from his point of view and no one else. He or she is unique in how they express this view to the world. All true art comes from observation and once an artist can "see" how they want to portray the world around them, then they use the tools that they are accustomed to using, whether it is paint, pencil, stone, or fiber.

Stephen's artwork has changed over the years, and lately is drawn to painting the different hues and light variations that are seen in nature.

He has also been inspired to create new and unusual still life paintings. While this has been done perhaps thousands of times before by various artists, each approach is new and different, and each approach has a new challenge of lighting and textural effects to capture.

Stephen is also focused upon spiritual subjects and longs to express this view of the world in Biblical and sometimes end-times scenes.

All-in-all his desire is to capture the scene or inspiration that is before him, and then to also invite the world into this scene so that they too, are caught-up in his inspirations.

Stephen now lives and travels full time in a travel trailer with his wife Carol who is also an artist. They have found that this life style gives them the freedom to devote to their artwork and to visit the many beautiful and unusual places around the country. Now they can also both spend time visiting their eight grand children as well.

Stephen is also the author of several other books that are devoted to prophecy and various other topics centered around his Christian faith and ministry.

One can view these books and visit his websites below.

Stephen Hanson~

www.hansonartists.com

www.stephenhansonprophet.com

STEPHEN HANSON

www.ingramcontent.com/pod-product-compliance
Lightning Source LLC
Chambersburg PA
CBHW051308220526
45468CB00004B/1253